T0131801

JOURNEY *into* HEALTH

HEAL YOURSELF WITH MEDITATION
AND THE AID OF YOUR SPIRIT GUIDES

KATRINA BLECHER
Hypnotherapist

BALBOA.
PRESS
A DIVISION OF HAY HOUSE

Balboa Press books may be ordered through booksellers or by contacting:

Balboa Press
A Division of Hay House
1663 Liberty Drive
Bloomington, IN 47403
www.balboapress.com
1 (877) 407-4847

Print information available on the last page.

ISBN: 978-1-5043-8336-3 (sc)
ISBN: 978-1-5043-8338-7 (hc)
ISBN: 978-1-5043-8337-0 (e)

Library of Congress Control Number: 2017910121

Balboa Press rev. date: 10/24/2017

To Heidi, with love. My sister, my healer, my friend.

Contents

Part I
Self-Hypnosis and Spirit Guides

Chapter:

Part II
Self-Healing

EMOTIONAL HEALING

Chapter:

PHYSICAL HEALING

Chapter:

Acknowledgements

I would like to thank my hypnotherapist, Ms. Heather Zicko, for helping me experience the wondrously healing and enlightening journey with my spirit guides.

I would also like to thank Patti Williams for her constant loving help and support. You are a marvelous person and I treasure our extraordinary friendship. You are forever in my heart.

Foreword

W hile there are plenty of books on hypnosis as a modality to improve and cure physical challenges, this book captures a unique viewpoint to health that very few have the expertise to write – the author encourages you to bring back health by utilizing universal energy and contacting your spiritual guides and protectors.

In 2016, I was a guest on Kate Blecher's Manhattan Neighborhood Network cable show *"Kates Holistic Healing"*, where she interviews holistic healers of different modalities for a 28-minute conversation. I later returned to the show to be the guest interviewer for Kate's own story. It was a story of immense perseverance through physical challenge, also shared in detail in her first book, titled *"Journey into Knowledge."* It is evident that as stated by the renowned philosopher Nietzsche, *"That which does not kill us makes us stronger"* rings very true for Kate's journey – a journey, which fortified her to have the strength to speak with authority in this book.

As a Vibrationalist, I understand that the Universal Force (aka Universal Energy, Original Life Force, and Original Energy Source) provides waves of energy at frequencies, called vibrations. In this book, Kate utilized the laws of vibrations to develop techniques and methods that she now shares with readers – ways to remove blockages to healing from both physical and emotional pain and to let love flow freely into the body and mind.

Kate presents her understandings with an honest, loving, and deep-seeded care for her readers. She has known most of her life that she would be "helping others". This work is her gift built from a lifetime of challenge that we can benefit from without enduring the pain and hardship she experienced. I found this book to be enjoyable and insightful, and just by reading it, it can change a life for the better.

By Laura Ferran
Founder of Vibrationalism

Episodes from *"Kate's Holistic Healing"* which first went on the air in 2014 can be seen online on YouTube at: Kate's Holistic Healing.

Introduction

This book is the result of the many conversations I have had with my spirit guides on how to fix a medical problem or disease. I have experienced and lived through over 40 medical conditions or diseases, from slight to terminal, and luckily, my spirit guides have been with me through them all. They have taught me how to cope with all sorts of feelings that accompany different types of illness, large or small. They have provided healing techniques that aided me in my quest for a healthier body and soul. Here I write about my experiences and share with you the plethora of knowledge and information I have received from my loving, healing, wonderful group of spirit guides. I hope that you will benefit from reading about them, apply what you learn to your own life and grow in the knowledge of self-healing through meditation and hypnosis.

I am proof that these techniques work (I survived four life-threatening conditions). My medical issues kept me bed-ridden (aside from doctor visits) for the better part of 10 years. Nevertheless, I am a complete fan of western medicine and I have an outstanding group of doctors. Just as important is that I have an exceptional group of holistic healers whom I see regularly. If you have a medical or emotional problem, I recommend seeing a doctor and practicing the meditation exercises in this book.

Unless otherwise indicated, the information in this book came to me while I was in a meditative trance, working with a hypnotherapist. Virtually all of the exercises in the book should be practiced during self-hypnosis and/or meditation. Although the two terms differ somewhat, for simplicity I use them interchangeably.

According to *American Health Magazine,* research has shown the following:

Psychoanalysis	**38% recovery**	**After 600 sessions**
Behavior Therapy	**72% recovery**	**After 22 sessions**
Hypnotherapy	**92% recovery**	**After 6 sessions**

Practicing these exercises while in a trance state induced by meditation has given me exceptionally positive results: I no longer use a walker, and I lead a relatively active, normal life. Another example of how these exercises have helped to improve my health is that I was able to reduce my pain medicine from seven pills a day to none and my anxiety medications down from 14 pills a day to 5. I feel so much better living without all the side effects of these medications.

I invite you to join me in the amazing world of self-hypnosis and self-healing. Here you will find that your spirit guides do not only guide you to inner knowledge about the natural healing process, but particularly for those who struggle with illness and pain and even terminal conditions, they have the ability to truly help you help yourself as you explore all avenues of healing through hypnotherapy. You too can be successful in living a more wonderful life than you could imagine despite medical and emotional obstacles in your way. This is the result of the boundless love from your guides and The Lord, as they help you find your correct path.

PART I

Self-Hypnosis and Spirit Guides

Chapter 1

Introduction to Self-Hypnosis

Welcome to the world of self-hypnosis – it is a skill instilled in us from birth. It is a completely natural state, as we drift in and out of trance throughout the day. When you are concentrating, watching TV or reading, you are frequently in a meditative trance.

Technically speaking, we experience several brain wave frequencies over the course of a day. When you are awake, your brain waves are in beta. When you are in a deep sleep, slower delta waves take over your brain. Theta brain waves dominate during self-hypnosis and light sleep. Theta brain waves are associated with a sense of deep spiritual connection and attachment to the universe.

Whether you are in good or bad health, the one activity you can always do is to play with your mind. What I find to be the most enjoyable is to practice self-hypnosis. Although I have found it is most productive when I am working with a hypnotherapist, doing it on my own while listening to a meditation recording is also an excellent experience. When I go into trance, I can ask questions of my spirit guides and receive abundant love and information in return. That is the beginning of true healing.

Beginners to Self-Hypnosis

All hypnosis is self-hypnosis. No one can make you do anything you do not want to do. A hypnotherapist will help ease you into a relaxed hypnotic state. Everyone can be hypnotized; the one caveat is that you must want to go into a trance. There is nothing to fear. At any moment, you can open your eyes and come out of trance.

Undertaking hypnosis is an excellent method to get to know your true self. You will come to be in touch with your real feelings and develop a strong connection to your body. Most importantly, you will develop a sense of self-love, bolstered by the constant love you receive from your spirit guides. In addition, you will have the ability to love others more easily and fully.

Meditation in my experience just makes life fabulous. As you get to understand your true self, you will find out what you are searching for, and what you really want. Getting to know yourself is an evolving process, because our desires change over time. When you meditate, you can ask about your wants and desires, explore your path in life and work toward your individual goals.

This book should help beginners feel less disconnected and adrift in life. They will be more in touch with themselves and other living things – not just going through life aimlessly but actually experiencing life to the fullest. When in a trance, they will feel love streaming from the cosmos, so much that it will make them tingle; they will never feel anything better.

Before you begin a meditation, it is helpful to set some ambience. Make the room as warm and welcoming as possible. Everyone should pick the items of comfort or familiarity that call to them the most. Perhaps burn some incense or candles. Dim the lights. Find a comfortable chair to recline on or lie down. Have a blanket handy, as people tend to get a bit cold during hypnosis.

The Spirit Guides

One of the most wonderful experiences you will ever encounter is the first time you meet your spirit guide. You will experience a strong and familiar connection with this spirit, one of overwhelming love. The best way to meet your guide is with the help of a certified hypnotherapist. Next best is listening to meditation recordings. I recommend the recordings of Dr. Brian Weiss, because he gently guides you to your spiritual awakening as he introduces you to your spirit guide. In addition, you can listen to meditations on YouTube from Kate's Holistic Healing, my own company. However, if you prefer to do it yourself, try the following exercise.

Allow your eyes to close and focus on your breathing. Let it be nice, easy breathing. Feel how your stomach rises and falls with each breath. Next, imagine you are standing at the top of a beautiful staircase. Slowly begin to walk down the stairs. With each step you take, you will go deeper and deeper into a relaxed and peaceful state. When you reach the bottom of the stairs, you will see in front of you a beautiful garden, full of flowers, grass, trees, fountains and places to rest. Go into the garden and find a place where you can relax.

Next, using your mind's eye, perform a body scan (see Chapter on Body Scans). Turn your attention to the crown of your head. Imagine a beautiful light and pick its color. The light will gently enter the top of your head. As you conduct the body scan using this light, your muscles will relax as it slowly moves down your body. Imagine the light permeating the muscles in your scalp, brain, eyes, jaw, neck, shoulders, and keep going down your body to get to the tips of your toes.

Then imagine that you are joined in the garden by someone very wise, loving and perhaps familiar to you in some way. That someone is your spirit guide. You can communicate with your guide. You can ask a question and listen for the answer. The answer may be in words, images, feelings or sensations. Keep asking questions and you will receive an answer. Keep listening and be patient. The answer will come to you and you will be surprised by the brilliance of the answers you receive. You should also keep a journal about what you learn in trance. If at any time you are feeling a bit down, you can re-read the messages of love from your guides.

I asked Costada, my spirit guide, what she would want beginners of hypnosis to know. Know that they are not alone, she said, and that they are very loved and cherished by their guides and The Lord. Those just beginning hypnosis may not yet feel connected to the cosmos, but that is because they are in a body, and no longer just a soul with the ability to communicate instantly with any other soul in the cosmos. However, they still are connected to higher powers.

Once you have met your spirit guide or guides, begin asking questions. Explore and take advantage of their knowledge. You will know you are receiving messages from your spirit guide, as the answers are different from the way you normally think. For example, once I was going on a very important job interview. I asked for advice about what I should do to ensure a good interview. Then I thought that was silly, as I knew I interviewed decently, was top ranked in my field and could intelligently field questions from potential employers. Nevertheless, I asked anyway while I was in trance and my guide said that during the interview, I should place my left hand over my right hand, and know my guide is with me holding my hands. This was not a thought I had ever had before, but it made sense and was one that I loved and employed successfully in the interview.

When you meditate, after you are relaxed and in trance, call in your guide(s). As mentioned, ask any and as many questions as you like. The more ways you ask a question, the more answers you will receive. I have found that sometimes the questions are as revealing as the answers. The following are some examples.

- What is special about what is happening with you right now?
- What is your message for the week or the month?
- How can you heal what is bothering you?

- Are you on your correct path?
- What do the guides or The Lord want you to do now?

If you cannot think of a question, meditate and imagine walking down a beautiful path. One by one, you come to three tables. On each table will be one item. What is the message of this item? How can it help you? Why is it there? Continue down the path to the second table and then the final table, asking questions about the item on each table.

Advanced Hypnosis Practitioners

After performing self-hypnosis for a while, it becomes second nature to go into a trance. You will find that the messages from your guides become clearer and more frequent. Once you are in a trance, and have completed a body scan, call to your guides and have them stand in front of you (they normally stand behind us or to our side). Begin asking questions and wait for the answers.

It is most productive to have your questions ready before you begin your trance. Always start a session of self-hypnosis with a body scan. You might find different areas of your body will shout out in pain. Do not ignore the pain. Ask your guides how to heal your physical discomfort. Throughout the book, I have addressed various medical conditions and have provided examples of solutions to medical/psychological issues.

After you have received a method to heal a problem, ask the question again but slightly differently. You will receive another technique to heal. You can ask general questions as well, such as these: What is the message this painful area has for you? Why are they telling you this message now? What is the meaning of the message? The same question, but each time you will get another answer, or what I call technique.

When I asked Costada what advanced hypnosis practitioners should do, she said that when they bring their spirit guides in, everything they need would already be in their circle. Their guides will tell them what they need and how receiving the message will help them.

The practitioners (while you are still in trance) should find out what will really solve your current issue by asking your guide. It is actually much better when you are advanced because then you can just ask your guides what you should know and they will tell you. It will all be good and come to you with clarity and large amounts of love.

When I asked my Arcturian guides what advanced people should know, they highlighted that the Arcturians are beings of love. They, or other angels, are always with you whether you speak to them or not. They love all people but guides are greatly drawn to those who are advanced – those who ask questions and desire knowledge. Then the guides can engage in enjoyable conversation. They are happy to be asked questions so that they can share their knowledge. They want to help you find your soul's path. The guides have said that people will be shocked at how easily life flows when you speak to your guides and live in the moment. My life completely turned around when I started talking to my guides on a daily basis. Now all is fantastic in my life.

I asked my Arcturian guides how someone knows when they've reached the advanced level. They believe it is when the person is very much in love with his/her guide(s) and knows that the guide is with them at all times. When a person can hear the messages clearly and easily in trance, then they are advanced.

You can also find out how to heal other people by asking the other person's guides for direction. Everyone has the ability to heal other people. If you are so inclined, you can have your guide ask another person's guide about a problem and how the other person can be helped.

An advanced person can tell the difference between their thoughts and messages from their guides. While someone is in trance, most of their thoughts are messages from their guides. They are not the same thoughts you have when you are awake.

A particularly encouraging message I received was that all should work out perfectly – that everything we need is already within our circle. People will start to see the solutions to various issues take shape and their world will improve dramatically, just as mine did. The things we need are available to us, and the things we need are the basics – air, water, food, companionship, love and shelter. These things are all around us; we do not need to search for them. The guides desire everyone to be happy; they supply virtually everything we need to be happy, to grow, and to love them.

Lastly, my guides say that the world of advanced people will turn around when they find deep self-love. It becomes easy to feel because the guides love us intensely and exactly as we are. They are very convincing, constantly reminding you how wonderful you are, so much that you have to start loving yourself as well. The guides will tell you there is no reason to dwell on past mistakes and there is no reason to be worried about the future. Focus on the present moment.

Do not worry; our guides are not judgmental and they will never say anything negative about us. What we consider wrong, they consider mild transgressions. They say we are very hard on ourselves, and that saddens them. The one exception is violence. Spirit guides do not understand the human desire to hurt one another and they wish that people would stop. Therefore, if you are a violent person, you should know that your guides do not like violence. We are all meant to be loved.

Major emotional problems may be the result of a negative experience in your childhood or it might be a holdover from a past life. Either way, hypnosis can help you find the cause of the problem through a regression. Once you relive the negative event, it ceases to be a major issue. You can then put it in the past, outside of your circle where it will no longer affect you.

Rapid Trance

Anyone can do a rapid trance, but realistically, a person has to have some experience with self-hypnosis. Try it, as it might work.

Step-by-step rapid trance:

- Get completely comfortable either sitting or lying down.
- Allow your eyes to close.
- Focus on your breathing.
- Feel the air moving in and out of your lungs.
- Do focused breathing three times, sinking deeper into the cushions with each breath. After the third breath say, "Deep Sleep," and you will feel your whole body sink into the bed or chair.
- Then do a body scan.
- Ask your guides questions and wait for the answers.
- When you are ready to come out of trance, count up from 1 to 5 before you come out. One, coming back to the room. Two, feeling wonderful, remembering everything you have learned in trance. Three, wiggle your fingers and toes. Four, feeling fabulous, feeling great. Five, open your eyes.

The benefits of a rapid trance include not having to spend time going deeper and deeper. In an instant, you can go right into trance and join your guides. When my guides are tightly squeezed up against me, I feel so protected and loved – and we all are.

The more you practice meditation the easier it is to do a rapid trance on the go. You can do this on the subway, while riding as a passenger in a car, or any time you can give yourself a couple of minutes to feel wonderful. Sit down and take three deep breaths. With each breath, sink deeper and deeper into the chair. Say to yourself, "On the count of three, my arms will be very heavy." Then count from one to three. Say to yourself, "When I open my eyes, I will feel wonderful, peaceful, fantastic, and full of joy." When you open your eyes, you will notice how great you feel and sense how heavy your arms are in your lap. Nevertheless, you will not care because you will be feeling great, and the heaviness does not last for more than a minute or two.

If your arms bother you, you can take three more breaths, go back into a trance and tell yourself that your arms in your lap feel very light as if they have balloons connected to them pulling them upward. When you open your eyes a second time, you will feel wonderful, peaceful and full of joy and your arms will be very light.

The guides have additional uses for the rapid trance. If someone is in a panic or nervous, maybe before giving a speech, it is a great way to ground and calm oneself quickly, which is very empowering.

Chapter 2

Introduction to Spirit Guides

My Spirit Guides

There are so many millions of spirit guides. You can feel their love surround you just through a simple gust of wind. The air that flutters past your body is full of love that does not end. You can take it all inside and your entire body will happily tingle. There is no lack of affection as your guides stand around you loving you so intensely.

Costada

When I first met Costada, my spirit guide, I felt immediate recognition and love. I knew she/he was my soul mate (souls do not have a sex to them, only bodies do). It was very powerful. She just looked in my eyes. I felt so cared for, as if for the first time. I was happy and astonished that somebody really thought I had value and it did wonders for my self-worth. She was the only guide I spoke to for the first 30 years of my meditating life. I find her very beautiful, with her amazing large green eyes and bald head. She is shorter than I am, wears a white robe and has a white glow about her. Her face glows with incandescent light as if from a low wattage light bulb. This glow goes beyond her body, so much that light thinly shines theatrically behind her, and in the shape of a radiant halo (some people say it looks like angel wings). She is very powerful, very gentle and knows all the answers.

I found her the first time by listening to the meditation recordings of Dr. Brian Weiss. Costada is all about making me happy and teaching me ways to improve my life experience. Most of all, she is about loving me. I have never received unconditional love like the love I receive from Costada.

Arcturian Guides

I met my Arcturian guides in 2012 (five of them, to be exact), when I took the course to become a certified hypnotherapist. When I first met them, they felt very familiar. I realized they had been there all along and I suddenly opened my eyes (metaphorically speaking as I was in a trance with my eyes closed) and saw them. They had been standing in a semicircle behind me all my life. Now I ask them to stand in front of me, in a circle around me, or in a circle with me. Sometimes, they stand crowded against me and keep me warm with their love. They help me with my balance, which is a challenge for me from having MS.

The Arcturians are in a higher dimension than Costada. They exude tranquility, power and intense love. In a more God-like manner, they speak about lofty ideas and ideals. The big picture is very important to them. Their ardent love of the planet and all of the souls that dwell within bodies is indeed constant.

Three of the Arcturians appear to be male and two are female. They are very tall. My head comes up to their rib cage. They have long beautiful hair and a warm glow about them. Their robes are mostly white but at times can be saffron-colored. The Arcturians tend to act and speak as one, except one of the females. She is always holding up a large, old-fashioned oval floor mirror, so I just see a reflection of myself. She says she is holding it to show me that I am part Arcturian. By telling me this, she assures me that I have as much power as they do when I am in lives between lives. I know that I always have the support of my guides and I never have to worry about being alone because we are so strongly connected.

Our guides are here to help us find our correct path in life. My path is to learn and to teach. Practically every day I learn something extraordinary from my guides. I am here to teach others and I am doing it already with my hypnotherapy practice, TV program, *Kate's Holistic Healing*, and the *Journey* book series. I can also heal my body when it needs healing. I know that I will join my guides after I die and that they love me purely and completely. Others can experience their own power by going into trance, talking to their guide(s) and asking what powers they have. I have no more or less power than anyone else. I just have spent a good amount of time in a trance.

John

When I met John, my beautiful red-tailed hawk animal spirit guide, I felt immediate love from him. A very pure love. He is a wonderful teacher. He has taught me to look to nature for answers. I love the fact that he is a red-tailed hawk because this type of hawk is considered the most spiritual of all animals. I am very proud of him.

When John stands next to me, he is up to my waist. He is a real character and he watches over me, especially at night when I sleep. In trance, he grabs hold of my backpack, and flies me over the land around us. He sends red-tailed hawks to our property at Kate's Holistic Healing Retreat Center, in Pawling, New York. I see them circling in the air, sitting in the trees and find their feathers on the ground. When I am in trance, John likes to perch on my toes when he is relaxing, but he is very heavy. He tends to nip at my toes. He said this is to bring circulation to my feet (I have Raynaud's, scleroderma and RSD in my toes). He likes to push his beak into my hand so I will pet his head. A few times, he has wrapped me in a big hug with his wings. It was so comforting.

Ralph

My second animal spirit guide is a big, old, wise, black bear. When I asked his name, he growled and then said "ph". It sounded like Ralph. When I asked if Ralph was his name, he laughed, and found the name very funny. Ralph is very bear-like. He does not talk about lofty ideas; he is all about keeping me warm and having fun. He likes it when I am in trance because then I ride on his back as he walks along. I have to hold onto his fur to keep from falling off him as he bounces along. At times when I ride him, I am my natural size and at other times, I am just a few inches tall (and then he is extremely bouncy). He has sent large black bears to my husband and me to protect us. He is always to the west of me. When I researched spirit animal guides, I saw that the bear is the animal of the west. Therefore, he is right where he should be. I asked why he was coming into my life right now, he answered, "Because he loves me." He is showing me all the beautiful things in nature. In addition, he is teaching me that I have to be adaptable. The more adaptable we become, the easier life will be.

Chapter 3

Body Scans-Ask Your Body What it Needs

W hen you want to heal any specific area, always begin your trance by relaxing and focusing on your entire body. You can do this by performing a body scan. The purpose of the scan is part relaxation and part healing. It allows you to check in with your whole body and see which areas, if any, need attention. In trance, if you have pain you will in effect hear that area of your body shouting out in pain. Ask the body part that wants attention what it would need to feel better. If a body part needs something that came to light during a scan, work on the problems as you come to them, or come back to them later – whichever feels correct. You can ask your guide what type of attention this area of discomfort needs. You should also ask if you should see a doctor, as my guides frequently tell me to do. In addition, you can address areas of discomfort by using the healing techniques in this book.

I have experienced and survived four terminal illnesses with the help of body scans, employing the techniques I learned from my guides, and with the help of a wonderful group of medical doctors – medical doctors who are at a loss to explain why I am doing so much better with my over 40 medical conditions (see About the Author). I know that the reason I am doing so much better is due to my immersion in holistic healing over the years, and listening to what my body says during my body scans.

How to Do a Body Scan

Like meditation, it is easiest to go into trance and do a body scan when you are working with a hypnotherapist or listening to a meditation tape. If you want to meditate on your own, go into a trance and conduct a body scan at the beginning of your meditation, as it will help deepen your level of trance.

You can do a body scan from the top of your head to the tips of your toes. Alternatively, do a scan from the tips of your toes to the top of your head. As you scan slowly from side to side, relax each area. First, for example, relax your scalp, brain, eyes, cheeks, jaw, neck, throat, shoulders, and down both arms. Relax your breathing, your lungs, and your heart; relax your organs, your upper and lower back, and your hips. Feel the muscles relax down each leg to the tips of your toes. Your whole body will feel peaceful and undisturbed, as you sink deeper into the surface beneath you.

I have done body scans and have identified problems long before I had the symptoms of my many diagnoses. Your body knows what is happening to it. I have had stage four cancer three separate times, each time a different cancer. In addition, I knew something was wrong with me for a year before I received a cancer diagnosis, twice. I am in remission from two cancers; the first one was over 10 years ago when I was informed that I had 1-2 years to live.

During another body scan, I felt one of my feet seemingly screaming out in pain. Since I had no pain while I was awake, it was confusing. A few months later, my foot started hurting, and it took a while to get a doctor to order me a scan (x-ray) of my foot. The scan showed that my foot was suffering from six stress fractures.

I had yet another body scan, this time starting at my fingertips. I realized I could not feel them. I have MS and so my hands are often numb. Consequently, I am frequently dropping things. I did not think my hands needed any healing, but when I asked the spirit guides about it, they said that a warm, healing, red cloud around my fingers during trance would bring in blood flow to heal them.

I continued my scan and when I reached my feet, I found out they needed attention too. The guides told me to wiggle my toes and fill them with healing orange light. My left foot is full of youthful energy and it does not have any pain left. My right foot is very happy because of the attention it has been getting. It too has the spirit of a teenager. I should remain focused on my feet and let them play.

At one point, I saw a stone on the ground. I picked it up to see the message written on it, which says "boots." I asked what that meant and my guides told me I was supposed to buy some boots so that I could walk in the stream on our property upstate. My youthful body is still inside me; I remember how much fun it was to walk in the stream when I was young.

Chapter 4

Dimensions, Frequencies, and Numbers

S pirit guides are very interested in different dimensions because as humans, we exist in a dimension that varies greatly from those of our guides. In addition, guides also travel through the various higher frequencies through which we can communicate with them.

Dimensions

The variety of dimensions is what captures the interest of our guides. This is because we, as humans, live in a three-dimensional world. Our guides, however, live in a far different, higher dimensional space. Dimensions can be likened to a flight of stairs; we just go up and down them, depending on which world we find ourselves in.

There is a period of life referred to as lives between lives in which we exist as souls in a different dimension. When we are just souls, in lives between lives, there is a beautiful light about us. This is the eternal light of our soul and the light is never extinguished. When we exist as humans with a body, this light is our aura.

When we are just souls, not only do we have a light about us but there is also a sound about us. Each of us has a name to our soul that is a beautiful melody. Our particular light and sound are not lost when we are in a body. As souls we might exist in a two-dimensional space, since light is two dimensional due to its infinite length. Alternatively, we might exist in a higher dimensional world. I tend to ask too many questions on this subject. My guides warn me not to think about it so much or I will just suffer headaches. However, it is pertinent information to know.

Humans are souls that have chosen to exist within a body, have a life experience on earth and live on a three-dimensional planet. As mentioned John, my beautiful red-tailed hawk spirit guide, and Ralph, my bear animal spirit guide, exist in this three-dimensional world – my world! Costada, my main guide and soul partner, is in the fourth dimension. The Arcturians exist in the fifth or sixth dimension. The Lord is everywhere, in every dimension, omnipresent.

Light

We are all familiar with flashlights, so try playing with one. Point it to the sky for a while and then turn it off. Know that the beam of light is still traveling and it will continue to travel in space for the rest of your life. As the light travels, we are not able to see the light beams. If you point the flashlight against the wall, you can see where it lights up the wall but you cannot see the beam of light itself. So all the souls of light and music, all the guides, are all around us; we just cannot see them, that is, unless we are in a trance. Angel readers can see our Angels/Guides and some people are able to see individual auras. Once when I was in a trance I opened my eyes and saw an aura around my healer. It was very beautiful.

According to physics, if we could travel at the speed of light we would not age. When we are souls, just beings of light, we are able to travel around the cosmos at the speed of light. This is one way we are able to enjoy eternity. According to my guides, this is the only explanation I am able to understand. Having a good understanding or a belief in the soul's separation from the body at death is very useful and can put you in a good frame of mind. This is because when we are once again just souls, and are home, we find that we indeed have all the knowledge that had been outside our grasp when we existed in a three-dimensional body on earth.

I asked what it was like to live in 4D, and the guides told me that 4D was out in another direction. Further, I asked what that meant, and they advised me not to think about it. I cannot understand 4D because I am stuck living in this three-dimensional world. However, the guides say that after we die, we can be guides to those souls in our circle that choose to have a bodily experience.

The only way we can encounter a different dimension is if we close our eyes and imagine two points. If we connect the two points with a line, we can then experience 2D. If you draw a line on a piece of paper, that is not 2D because you can see the length and width and know that a thin layer of ink was laid down (depth). Therefore, it is only with our minds that we can cross from one dimension to the next. This is why we can communicate with our guides in a trance. However, I believe that our guides are psychic and do not actually need to speak at all.

Frequencies

Frequencies are important because they are the conduit by which we are able to communicate with our guides. Do not forget music. Spirit guides love when we dance and sing. Importantly, music has frequencies attached to it. When we concentrate and really listen to music, the theta brain waves allow us to experience a trance-like state. We are able to relax, remain calm and stay deeply connected to our spirit guides.

I once heard the most wondrous sound while in a deep trance. No vocals or instrumentals, just a hauntingly beautiful melody. Years later, Costada said that music was my true name. All our true soul names are beautiful, unique melodies. Therefore, whenever I ask my guides their names, their answers are quite witty since they know that I know their true names are melodies.

In addition to music, color plays an important role in communicating with our guides. Each color has a different frequency. Our guides say that we understand color better than we understand frequencies. Always focus and really see the color you are working with. I recommend going into a trance and imagining your body is filled with a color. Then wait for the resultant feeling or sensation. Go through each color so you can experience and really feel the differences.

When you find the correct color (or colors) let the color envelop you. Then wear the color(s) that you find the most appealing. They are your power colors and provide the frequencies you need. You will know which colors are good for warmth, love, or happiness. Your correct colors have frequencies that can also be very healing. Various colors will have a different impact on each individual. Do not underestimate the power of each frequency. Think about your wardrobe. What is the most common color? What was it 7 years ago? What was it 14 years ago?

Seven is an important number, because we grow in seven-year increments. Look at your life in seven-year increments. Most of our cells turn over every seven years, so it is as if you are a completely new person every seven years. Where were you 7 years ago? Think about where you were 14 years ago or 21 years ago and see how you've changed. See what you have accomplished, and see how you have grown. Be proud of yourself.

Sequins offer a unique way of looking at color. My guides use them because sequins have so many facets of color; they not only have a color, but also reflect color. Guides like it when we go into a trance, because we become more reflective. It is how we can help ourselves grow.

To the guides, vibrations and frequencies are the same thing. Imagine that you have a little bell and you hit it. The bell then sends out sound waves like ripples upon a lake. It is the same with varying frequencies, and this allows people to talk to each other without words. They say frequencies are the most important because we are vibrating at all times. Each cell is vibrating. When our vibration is low people tend to shy away from us, and when our vibration is high (in a good mood) we attract people. That is why depressed people tend to live a more solitary existence.

You can change your vibration as easily as changing your shirt. As soon as you put on another colored shirt, you experience another vibration. Consider keeping a journal about how your day is going depending upon what colors you wear. The one color that is good for everyone is a bluish-white light, like the color of the sky on a bright cloudy day. The energy for the radiant blue-white light is derived from all the souls and from The Lord. We radiate light. The aura is the light of our souls, which is why our skin is not where we stop. We have a glow about us but the guides have much more of a glow. Their skin looks like a low wattage light bulb. One of the reasons they say they do not need to have thick skin is because guides do not get sick often (as humans, skin is our number one defense against illness). That is why their soul light shines through and makes them look like they are glowing.

Numbers

Excerpts taken from http://sacredscribesangelnumbers.blogspot.com

Numbers are also important. I did a meditation on different numbers and the colors associated with them. I picked my favorite numbers, 3, 6, and 9. The number 3 made me feel light and airy. Its color to me was blue.

Number 3 "resonates with the energies of optimism and joy, inspiration and creativity, speech and communication, imagination and intelligence, compassion, energy, expansion, and the principles of encouragement, assistance, a love of fun and pleasure, brave, psychic ability, manifesting and manifestation."

Number 3 "works with the energies of the Ascended Masters, and indicates that the Ascended Masters are around you, assisting when asked. The Ascended Masters help you to focus upon the Divine spark within yourself and others, and assist with manifesting your desires. They are helping you to find peace, clarity and love within."

Number 6 is "related to the vibrations and energies of unconditional love, balance and harmony, home and family, selflessness, nurturing, empathy and sympathy, emotional depth, honesty and integrity, protection, healing, solution-finding, seeing clearly, teaching, curiosity, peace, reliability, and providing."

When I felt Number 9, I experienced feelings of strength and the color green. I turned it into a cloud because the green wanted to encircle my whole body. It's like Chi. It makes me feel movement and makes me feel strong.

Number 9 is "the number of Universal love, eternity, faith, Universal Spiritual Laws, karma, spiritual enlightenment, spiritual awakening, service to others, leading by positive example, philanthropy, a higher perspective, loyalty, discretion, brilliance, problem-solving, inner-wisdom, self-love, high ideals, tolerance, humility, empathy, perfection, mysticism, optimism and Divine wisdom."

I then went on to go through all the numbers, the color they related to and the emotion associated with them. It was a fascinating exercise and one I highly suggest trying. This is done to gain information. This is a healing exercise, as it lets you know yourself better.

We also have the ability to sense energy. This is a fascinating exercise, if you did not know you could sense energy. For example, place your hand just above a new leaf and then an old leaf. See if you can feel the difference. The new leaf should be lighter feeling. This technique can be used to determine if a pill, food or other item is positive or negative to your body. Simply place the food or item in your hand and see if what you sense is its energy. Then pick up another food and see if you can feel the difference. With a little practice, you will learn how to sense which items your body wants, and it's not always what your head says you want. (Please see Chapter on Weight Loss, How to determine if a food is good for you.)

The healing power of the sun is the most powerful healing agent we have on the planet, according to the Arcturians. Close your eyes and put your hand up to the sun. You can feel the energy of our star. The sun makes everything grow – and as we grow, we heal. Sunlight is very important. The body needs it. We are even able to create a vitamin out of it, Vitamin D. So work on sensing energy, it will improve with practice and it is very empowering as your learn new skills.

Chapter 5

Angels

My guides do not speak of "Angels" as they do not recognize the word. In their view, many of our words, especially our names, are simply wrong. As mentioned before, our eternal soul names are not words at all but instead are strikingly beautiful melodies. We can call our guides angels but this word is incorrect. The guides, however, do not mind being called angels. The word is the problem, not the concept. English, unfortunately, is a very limited way of communicating.

My angels do not have wings; the light behind and above them is their soul light, their aura. According to my guides, some people have mistaken these for wings. In the Bible, angels do not have wings.

The Arcturians are a certain race, but they are not human. They are a type of angel. There are angels from all over the cosmos. How are Arcturians different from other angels, I inquired one day? The guides say they are a high level of angel. They say I am at a high level too. My guides and my hypnotherapist say that I am part Arcturian. Not everyone has Arcturian guides but everyone does have angels.

Some guides have had human experiences. They have also had life experiences on other planets. This is because they can cross into different dimensions. They laugh at our idea of spaceships. They say we travel by lives, not spaceships.

Chapter 6

The Future & The Past

We look at the future all wrong, according to my guides. We talk about the past, present and future, as if they are three separate and equal concepts. When I asked my guides what comes to mind when they think of the future, they replied, "The present. There is no future. It is just a moment we have not yet reached. It doesn't exist because it hasn't happened yet." There is no point in thinking about it as it is just a figment of our imagination. It is like walking up the hill and imagining what it looks like on the other side. You miss all the beauty around you when you should be enjoying the present moment. Instead, when you get to the other side of the hill, you can enjoy that "future" moment in the present.

I found this quite interesting. I asked if animals think about the future. To some degree they do, because they store food for the winter. However, this is a natural move for them. When I asked if there is anything instinctive about us regarding the future, wasted time and energy was the answer. While it is prudent to prepare for the future, we should know that the future will take care of itself just as each moment does. You can envision the future, yet realize that it is always going to be different from your expectations. My guides are not fans of the future; they just care about the present moment.

When I inquired about the future, I came across three leaves. Each one had a word on it about the future. "Past" was written on the first leaf. The word was on the underside of the leaf so it had already happened and I was told not to pay much attention to it. "Future" was written on the second leaf. I was informed it is just a word on the bottom of the leaf. It had no substance. "Joy" was written on the third leaf. In this moment, I was advised I was full of joy. Everything was fading away except the present moment.

I asked about light travel and it was explained to me that it is like a planet rotating around the sun. It just goes straight and then the magnetic energy of the cosmos pulls it, so light travels in a sort of orbit around the cosmos. Our souls have a light to them. This means that we are endless and just go on forever. This is the eternal nature of our souls. On other planets, inhabitants know about the light of souls and light travel. We have to teach the people when they are ready to learn.

There is no such thing as time travel. Time is just a concept. It is just the next moment. The guides really do not think that there is much reason to focus on it. After all, why would we want to time travel? We have already lived the past and the future is out of our control.

A way to engage with the present moment, is to stand with your feet apart, no trance required (never go into a trance while standing because you will fall over, unfortunately, I know this from firsthand experience). Concentrate on each different sense. What do you hear? Feel? Smell? See? Focus on now; do not think about the past and future. If you, like me, have a poor memory, you will be more likely to remember this experience. See what messages you receive. When I am in the moment, I am getting better, feeling younger and completely happy.

PART II
Self-Healing

EMOTIONAL HEALING

Chapter 7

Emotional Pain

I t is harder to deal with emotional pain versus physical pain because the former can involve somebody else and his or her feelings for you. Thus, it is partially out of your control, which makes it more difficult. Emotional pain can also be worse than physical pain. Just look at the very depressing statistics on suicide. It is not a very common practice to commit suicide due to physical pain.

To heal emotional pain, go into a trance and call in your guides. Rather than have your guides stand behind you in a semicircle, put your guides and yourself around a little circular table so you can hold their hands or they can put their arms around you.

To deal with emotional pain you need to go back to where it started. You do this by identifying the pain you want to address and thinking back to when it began. It may be from childhood or a holdover from a prior life. If you cannot remember, you should be able to remember in trance. Relive the event, repeatedly, until you make it a non-event. This will stop it from being something you are afraid to look back on. Writing about the negative event is also very good therapy. You can make your writing as detailed as you want, but the goal is to make it honest. You will find that when you re-read your story in the future, it will have less of an impact on you.

When you determine what hurts, remember whether there was a person involved in causing that hurt. If there was, see if there is any truth to the painful memory. If there is no truth to the memory, then you can ignore it. If there is some truth, you need to relive the event until it is no longer hurtful or triggers any fright in remembering it. At this point, you should then begin to learn the lesson connected to this event. When dealing with your spirit guides you will determine that there is always a lesson to be learned. Once you do, you can forget about the painful memory and remind yourself that the memory is part of the past and does not need to affect your life today.

If a person caused this pain, again remind yourself that it is in the past. In order to let go of the pain fully, you somehow have to find forgiveness. Find the pain. Find out where it came from. Get through it with repetition. Then forgive the person who hurt you. If you want to overcome the emotional pain, you have to be willing to let the hurt from someone else dissipate.

The easiest way to forgive a person is to go into a trance and remember three good times you had with the person who hurt you. If you can do this, it will make you remember that the person really does have positive feelings for you. The pain will go away because you remember that the underlying emotion is love.

Fear and love are usually at odds with each other. If you let more love in, there is no room for emotional pain. Try to re-experience the love of the person who hurt you. Remember that you would not have been hurt so badly if this person were not important to you. If a stranger on the street insults you, you usually don't care; but with someone you know, if you do not get past the pain, the relationship will never heal. You do not need anything from the person who hurt you. If the other person will not or cannot participate, it is irrelevant. It is your pain, and you can choose to toss it away. However, if the person touches on a sensitive area because it is true, you can try to fix it.

In my guides' opinion, it does not make a lot of sense to confront the person who hurt you. You should just repair the relationship yourself or you could end the relationship, whichever is healthier. Sometimes it is just all about the other person. Commit to stop dwelling on painful memories. Painful memories need not be a part of your life. According to the wise Arcturians, frequently negative, hurtful comments say more about the speaker than about you.

How do we know if something said about us by another person is true? According to the guides, we all know the truth on some level; however, when people point out what they perceive to be our faults, it hurts. Fortunately, the guides do not see us as having faults. What we view as mistakes, they consider mild transgressions.

There are times that people feel so much emotional pain that they do not want to live anymore. That is their choice. If they die, they just go back into the beautiful collective soul world. However, it might be a shame to waste the rest of your life just because you are at a low point. Therefore, you should look behind you at all the hills and mountains you have overcome in your life. Look at all the progress you have made, and remember that you can overcome your current emotional pain.

If you do not know why you hurt and cannot pinpoint the problem, it might just be generalized depression. Nevertheless, there is always a trigger. Use meditation and go back to the root of the pain. It is very important not to carry the pain over into the future. We do not need to suffer unnecessarily. Our guides say that we suffer needlessly a lot.

One way to avoid the pain is to call in your guides. Ask them to surround you in a very tight circle. Feel their intense love. That can remove most emotional pain.

A trance for releasing emotional pain

Once you are in a deep, comfortable trance, visualize the person who said something that deeply hurt you. Recall the words accurately. If there was some truth to it, thank the person who said it even though the words hurt your feelings.

In a trance, begin to take all the feelings of emotional pain out of your body and direct them towards a sphere, rolled up into a ball of pain. Imagine the sphere is colored tan. In front of your face, hold up the little tan sphere. Keep directing the painful feelings towards the ball by exhaling all the pain into the ball. Keep blowing patiently and steadily, increasing the size of the ball and darkening the color towards brown. Eventually there will be a huge ugly brown sphere of pain. Then after you have remembered all the pain, all the little childhood issues, all the useless insults, blow on the sphere, and push it away from you. Keep blowing until it reaches the horizon. At the horizon, it explodes in a burst of light and disappears. It is no longer in existence; it is in the past, which is behind you. So let it go with love, as it disappears.

We can also release emotional pain through physical activity. Hug yourself long and hard and imagine that you are hugging the person who hurt you. Call in your spirit guides. They radiate such love in their messages that it makes the pain dissipate. How can you be depressed when you have the intense love of your spirit guides and an eternal soul made up of light and love? Determine the exact point of the pain in your body and in your brain and try some magic spackle on it (please see chapter on Neurological Issues). Alternatively, you can even brush the memories away with a magic brush.

My guides said I was keeping myself closed off from some emotions, people, pain and experiences. I need to take risks and open myself up to more emotions. My goal is to learn not to be afraid, to open myself up to my true feelings and to be receptive of other people's feelings– literally to let all the emotions out and in. This is my one of my goals. I can do it now because I know I have the help and love of my guides.

Chapter 8
Emotional Stability

I n terms of emotional stability, it is good to stay in the middle of the bell-shaped curve – neither depressed nor fearful nor manic. The guides believe that people go through wide emotional swings that can hurt your emotional well-being but also that there are methods to bring one back in balance to his/her center. Your emotional aim should be joy, love, happiness, peace and bliss. All are high-level emotions. This is not easy to achieve all the time, but just as we can regulate our body's temperature, we can also regulate our moods. It just takes practice.

It is necessary for good health that we connect to ourselves emotionally. The spirit guides admit that this is hard for us, but a connection will keep us from going away from our center and into a depression. The guides advise us to seek out feelings that are normal to happy, but nothing beneath normal. Do not become scared and do not get manic. If you find you are experiencing these feelings, meditate and call in your guides. You should be able to feel their love and protection. Next, ask how you can overcome your current negative situation or mood.

Maintaining emotional self-stability is important because it is very easy to make a wrong turn and find yourself in a downward mental spiral. It is necessary to keep yourself centered. The guides believe this is so important because when you are centered you know you have a starting point that gives you purpose and a sense of balance and even peace.

To be centered you must concentrate on your thoughts – stop and think about what they are and where they are coming from.

Compare them to reality. If they are negative thoughts, stop them. I cannot stress enough the importance of taking control of your thoughts. Meditation can be a key and effective way to achieve emotional stability. By going into trance, you will be able to curtail your negative thoughts. There is no depression and no fear in a meditative trance state, just as there is no depression or fear during sleep.

I recently found myself in a very unhappy, anxious state. I listened to my guides and tried to figure out the cause of my sudden fear. It took some time. I lead a relatively quiet life and spend my days with my husband. However, I knew I was scared. It finally dawned on me that I had jury duty in a couple of days and I was afraid of traveling to the courthouse myself, finding the appropriate room and being on my own with strangers for an unknown number of days. As soon as I realized why I was scared, my trepidation went away. I remembered all the times I did jury duty in the past without incidence. I also knew I would have no trouble finding the proper location. No pills or discussions with a psychiatrist could have yielded me better results. So remember we can control our thoughts. It takes more effort than taking a pill, but the positive results will not wear off.

If you do not have time to go into a trance, always have a positive thought or memory at hand so when you start to get down you can focus on the happy memory. This could be any happy memory: the birth of a child, a wedding engagement or any time you were the center of attention, and loving it.

Our guides believe that we are unreasonably hard on ourselves. There should be no self-recrimination. In a very positive way, they think we are doing a wonderful job at life. We take care of so many good things. An exception, however, is violence. Our guides want us to avoid violence at all costs.

Chapter 9

Overcoming Anger

If you are angry with someone, ask your guides if you should stay angry or if you should forgive them. Once you decide to forgive, ask how you should go about it. When I meditated on anger, it came up that I was still angry with a very close friend. I asked if I should forgive her or stay angry. I felt that if I forgave her, it would be like giving her a gift she does not deserve. She had been nasty to me for many years.

When I went deeper into trance, three flowers were shown to me. The first one was a violet, with three petals – two lavender and one yellow. I could take the yellow petal and throw it away, but I would then be much sadder. I see now that I would have been much happier if she (the petal) stayed attached. I realized I did not want to pull off the yellow petal. Just as I realized I did not want to remove her from my life.

The second flower was a yellow tulip. Its message was that we are not going to be here forever and I should appreciate this friend while I have her. Pushing her away was not the solution.

The third flower was a red rose. It represented how to forgive and release hurt embedded in your heart. I was told to look deeply within the dense petals. If there was something that I didn't like, I could just pick that one petal and throw it away. I could pick out the bad things she did and throw them away. I did so and then they were outside my energy field and harmless (actually my spirit guide John wanted to pick them out). John is a great protector. My heart had hurt before, but it doesn't now.

Next, I saw the flowers melded together. It was a much happier picture than the violet with one petal taken off. It's great to have these two pictures to compare and contrast. There was no anger left because I took my friend's positives into my heart, and tossed away the rather small things she did that hurt me. She is back in my life and she never knew how she hurt me. The pain is gone, because I decided I wanted to keep her close.

Chapter 10

Self-Love – Body Image – Self-Worth

I f you have a strong sense of self-love, you are golden. However, some people do not view themselves with love. That needs to be worked upon, as self-love is a major theme taught by my guides.

One needs to have a positive sense of who they are and where they are in the universe. People should be very connected to their spirit guides. They will help heal you and improve every area of your life. Furthermore, our guides really want us to communicate with them so we can be on our correct life path. Once you start asking questions of your guides and receiving loving answers, your life will vastly improve in many ways.

External Self-Worth

According to my guides, self-worth is the opinion you have of yourself and your place in the world. It should be complete love. If it is not, you have to work on it because there is little that is more important than self-love.

The basic steps to increasing your self-worth are twofold: One is for your exterior and one is for your interior. You can increase your exterior self-worth by looking at yourself in the mirror. There are areas that you see that you might not like, but look at them closely and realize they are a part of you. Moreover, realize that you love them. They are a gift from The Lord to you.

If you do not feel the love while you are looking at yourself, keep redoing the mirror exercise until you feel the love. If there is a part you do not like, realize it is a part of you and you will love it. You might feel better about yourself if you put some cream on the part you are not happy with, possibly a wrinkle remover (I recommend *Immuderm*) if that is what's bothering you as you look in the mirror. On a more serious level, if you have any type of cancer, like I have had, you have to accept, and love, that part of you simply because it is you. Moreover, cancer cells are just tiny damaged cells. Acceptance of your physical body is not enough; you have to love your body.

Internal Self Worth

To increase your self-worth on the inside, use a face mirror. Look in your eyes. Stare at your eyes. Get to know yourself. Go through all the wonderful things you have accomplished. Be proud of these endeavors.

Meditate about a tree you are going to climb. At the top of this tree, you are going to have a different perspective on self-worth. Each branch you come to will have a message for you.

I undertook this exercise and received the following insightful messages. The first branch said, "Love yourself." It was written in magic marker, the words just appeared on the branch. The message meant I should stop beating myself up for what I am not doing. My actions are not bad; I am actually doing good things. We spend too much time focusing on negative actions. Change and make a list of all the good things about yourself.

Costada, my wonderful guide, suggests that everyone should go through a list of all the negatives in the past. Then move past it. Remind yourself of why you did these things and know that you have not done anything terribly wrong. There is no point in dwelling on past mistakes. They are in the past and out of your control.

On the second branch, I find my hypnotherapist, Ms. Heather Zicko. She is small in stature and she is dancing in a circle on the branch. The message here is that it feels like we are going round and round and there is nothing wrong with that. It is the way it is supposed to be. We are just re-learning the same things. Not making mistakes, as we tend to believe. For anyone to be alive, they have had to accomplish a lot in their lives. Ask your guides to help you if you cannot think of what you have accomplished in your life.

When you note the negatives, you can toss them away. Just fling them away, outside of your energy circle. Cut off all ties so the negatives can never find their way back. Make it a final, real separation.

When I reached the third branch, it said, "Swimming is good". The reason is to return to water. We are meant to spend more time in water, because we came from water in our mother's belly. I noticed that it was raining and all the animals were out. It's great to wash the body. Everything there just drips off with the water. Everyone should spend more time in water. Let your skin absorb it. This ties back to self-worth since we will see more of our body and we will love ourselves more.

The fourth branch said, "Keep climbing". The guides like the idea of me climbing a tree. The tree is welcoming me. The message I get is when we feel better, we are welcomed more by the world and other people.

My guides said that when I reached the top of the tree I would have a new perspective of self-worth.

When I got to the top of the tree, it said that I was God (I found that interesting, because I am clearly not God). My guides explained that it is true because The Lord is in all of us (Christianity calls it the Holy Spirit). We should all feel like a part of Him. They said The Lord is right beside us and in every cell. Talk about self-worth, what could be better than feeling like a part of The Lord?

How can we remind ourselves that we have God within us? Be still and you will just know. He never lets us go. We are always a part of him. It was a great tree to climb. Meditate, climb a tree and see what messages appear on your branches. I was told to remind myself of my worth by putting lotion on, stretching, hugging myself, dancing and twirling.

Practical Applications for Self -Worth

Step 1

Make a list of what you don't like about yourself. In the same manner of getting rid of negative emotions you can get over negative thoughts on self-worth. Look at the part of you that you don't love. Realize that it's part of you. How can you not love it, when you are so loved by your guides and God? We should forget everything in the past that we didn't like, and realize it's over. Be forgiving of yourself. Just let the negative thoughts float away. Imagine watching them as they drift further and further away, over the horizon.

Next, make a list of what you love about yourself. Always ask your guides if you need help. Repeat this list to yourself. Know you can accomplish anything. Everything you need is within your circle already. Using daily affirmations are also beneficial.

Step 2

Take a long, soothing shower to relax or awaken your senses. Take a bath to nurture your body and to feel refreshed and alive. Put on lotion to sooth your skin, to show yourself some love and reduce stress. Look at yourself in the mirror. Be proud of all you are, including your body. This is your body for this lifetime, only. Each life, we receive a new body, so don't dwell on any negatives concerning your body. The guides feel that vanity is a waste of time. Even though I have had so many illnesses that have taken their toll on my body in terms of scars and the like which I thought made me look bad, I now love my body (even my painful, active bone tumors).

How to Improve Self-Love

When I did the exercise to improve self-love, I received messages from three different stars. They said everything is connected. The stars are important, and I am just as important as the stars. There is a synergistic energy that I can feel as it bounces from me to the stars and from the stars back to me.

During one session, while I was staring at the night sky in a trance I encountered three stars. The first star said, "I love you. You are home. You're a part of us."

The second star I encountered said that it loves me and it wanted me to visit again. It said I had been there before. It told me not to forget the importance of music. Music is vital to us, in all dimensions. So if you do not have music in your life, bring it in and see how it makes you feel.

The third star appeared to be a much smaller star because it is much farther away. It said it loves me and that I am home. It is so very glad that I connected to this great star. This is the star I am connected to the most and this is the star that looks down and watches over me all the time. It is one of my true homes. I've been there many times. I asked if my guides came from there but my guides come from the entire cosmos. The guides are light and they just dance around the cosmos. We all dance around the cosmos, having fun, during our lives between lives.

Next, I am sitting in a circle with all of my guides holding hands. They said this beautiful star has so much love for me. The light inside my body is like the light of the star. It is as if my heart is connected. My guides said the connection is so strong that I can virtually just stretch out my arm out to the star. I asked my guide Costada if this is where she lived, and she said she lived with me and she also lived there. She was very glad I found it. She suggests everyone should find his or her star.

To find your own star go into a trance. Imagine lying down and looking at the peaceful night sky above you. With your eyes closed, look up and feel the energy coming from the stars. In your mind's eye, find a bright star. Ask the star what message it has for you. Then try another star. Let yourself relax even more and see if there is one star in particular calling out to you. It may move a little closer to you and you may feel a tremendous calling. The energy starts to flow between you and the star. You realize it is watching over you all the time. Even in the daytime, the star is still connected to you. You have found your star. It loves you. You can ask it questions, and it will answer you.

Adaptability is another wonderful skill we should encourage. Each morning when you wake up, you start with a clean sheet. You should know what you are capable of doing and what you are not. Then you must accept what you are not able to do, without regret. You have to be aware of your limitations. You can do quite a bit despite these limitations; you just have to find a way around them. With practice, you can become an expert at this. There is such enjoyment when looking at a problem and finding a solution. We can all find our own solutions, but doing it in trance is more productive.

Do not make your to-do list for a super hero. Rather write down what you want to accomplish that day. Pick the three most important and circle them. Then pick the one you will do first.

When you have completed that chore, be proud of yourself. One chore a day should be sufficient for you to feel productive and proud. Then do something that will be good for your happiness.

Our souls are eternal. When we are not in the state of lives between lives, we might choose to take an adventure in bodily form. The body we choose houses our eternal soul. Our body is a gift from God. Our spirit guides want us to appreciate and take good care of this gift bestowed upon us. Today, with great emphasis on health and exercise, this does not mean we have to kick into high gear and hit the gym daily. Instead, we can spend time emulating the animals. Try not to work endlessly, and incorporate play and movement into your daily routine without putting stress on your body. Stroll around; do not rush or sit.

In terms of our individual activity levels, my guides tell me that we may feel that we are not active enough or that we waste time procrastinating. Actually, you can accomplish a great deal when you just sit still and spend time thinking about and working through your issues. Guilt has no place here although we may not see tangible proof of our efforts. We can see large changes in our life over time, as our outlook brightens with the endless love and support of our guides. I have never known my guides to be wrong. In their view, we put too much pressure on ourselves – it is all self-induced.

"Slow down, you move too fast" – Art Garfunkel and Paul Simon were on to something with "*The 59th Street Bridge Song*". There is no need to rush. However, there is a need to slow down, because you miss so much if you rush through every day of your life. We should all live life with more ease, fewer deadlines and less worry. Yes, we may have work, home responsibilities, children or elderly parents to tend to – there are many calls upon our time that cause us to rush from one thing to another. Nevertheless, we must force ourselves to stop. A moment spent worrying is a moment wasted and one that might be used to enrich our lives, make us mindful of something important to us and simply allow us to discover peace. An excellent goal is to appreciate every moment. Take time to be good to yourself. Minutes do not matter in the grand scheme of life.

We are all surrounded by an aura, a halo of light. Our skin is only part of our being. Our essence goes beyond our skin. That is why hugging works so well to calm someone's anxiety. A hug allows you to tap into someone else's energy level. Actually, we are hard-wired from birth to find comfort in a hug.

I saw a mother at her car in the parking lot. She put her baby into the car seat in the back. Then she closed the door and the baby started to cry. So she opened the door, took him out of his car seat, hugged him and he stopped crying. Know that you have the power within yourself to help another when they are upset or anxious. Just give them a big, long hug. You should also hug yourself, and know your guides are hugging you as well.

Please see Chapter on Scleroderma for "Example of how to show love to a body part."

Chapter 11

Death and the Following Moment

We all wonder what exactly will happen right after our death. Do we cross over somewhere? Does our journey continue? Do our souls really separate from our bodies and live on? Or, is there simply nothingness? These are all fascinating questions. Given my serious medical history, I have thought about death often. Thankfully, I have my guides with me. I have asked my different spirit guides what happens after death. After calling them in, I am tightly surrounded by Costada, my five Arcturian guides and my animal spirit guides, John and Ralph. They have given me my answers. Below I describe what you should do to find out the answer for yourselves.

As usual, start with self-hypnosis. When you are in a deep trance, ask your spirit guides to tell you what happens the moment following death. I have done this exercise a number of times and am no longer fearing death. When death comes, I was told that I should call on my relatives who have passed on. The guides say that as soon as I die, my relatives will be waiting for me.

I asked for more information. I was told that everything goes from being dark to being light. There is freedom. You can float. You can just float above your body and it feels good because there is no pain. It is a very easy separation; your soul just drifts up and leaves your body while your physical body stays at rest. You can look down and see your body at rest. You know that you just died. Best of all, you are home again.

Previously I mentioned the bluish-white light of souls. After one passes on, your soul exists in a beautiful blue/white world and everyone you have loved, and who has passed over, is there. My guides are there too. We can still play. The more advanced we are, the more we see the importance of playtime.

After we die, we can go anywhere we want to go. We might decide we want to zip around the cosmos because it is fun, and communicate with the people we meet as we travel through time. We are beings of light, love and music. In addition, we get together with all the people we love just by thinking about them. Costada said there is no afterlife. There is just life. We just leave our body and return home.

I asked Costada what happens in a near death experience. She said there was no such thing. You either are in a live body or are just a soul. Nevertheless, people do come back from being dead. They see the same thing. They see the light. They see all the people waiting to welcome them back. They go above their body, and they remember everything.

My guides said there is no real purpose in reviving someone whose heart has stopped. They say human dislike of separation is the reason why we see a need to bring people back. The only people who want to bring them back are the humans who are still there. In reality, there is nothing wrong with letting them die. People who pass on are happy in their true home; they are still here but in a different dimension.

Costada said that it is often frustrating to be a spirit guide. At times when a spirit guide loves a soul that is within a body, there is often no communication between the spirit guide and the person. The guides try to give us messages, but we do not always listen. Spirit guides use our instincts to give us messages in addition to conversing with them in trance. Luckily, my guides are very happy with me because I talk to them regularly and I listen to their messages (I see a hypnotherapist weekly). We constantly have loving, protective, spirit guides with us. We should be more open to their messages as they attempt to reach us.

Messages are communicated psychically. You just need to think a thought and the guides can understand, just as you can understand their thoughts. Communicating with your guides is an excellent practice. Ask about the end of your life on earth and you will get answers – and not just words but emotions as well. As soon as you die, all the questions go away. You do not have to wonder about things. You remember all the answers. You know exactly how the cosmos works. In addition, you know how everyone is feeling. When the hypnotherapist asked why someone would be unhappy, Costada replied that we are only unhappy when we are in a body. We cannot be unhappy when we are just perfect souls because we are so close to God.

After death, you can see many points of light coming from all the souls. The Arcturians are saying we do not ever die, and that we have been around since the beginning. Currently, we are living on a very, very primitive planet.

Costada wanted me to communicate to people that there is nothing to be afraid of regarding death. The guides, of course, believe that we should look forward to death. In death, all the negative things just fall away. You do not miss the people you leave because in a short time, they too will die and rejoin you. Additionally, one can be around them as a spirit guide while they are alive.

One way for a living person to communicate with someone who has passed on is to see a reputable psychic. They also say you can talk to anyone when you are in a trance. Everyone has some form of psychic ability. Some people call them instincts. It is so much better when we are just souls. We do not have to worry about what people think of us because it is all out in the open and it is all good.

When we are souls, we are already advanced. Therefore, we come into these bodies so we can have experiences of growth. I believe there are few challenges when we are souls so there is not the same ability to grow.

We are supposed to grow through this lifetime. We naturally have tendencies to grow. We work through problems, overcome bad habits and help others. I asked if there was a specific purpose in this life for me. I was told I had to grow and had to find self-love. I am here to learn and to teach other people about their guides and life after death. According to my guides, at some level, everybody knows the soul continues after death.

They say it is harder to be born than it is to die. Both experiences are natural, but death is easier and everyone is waiting to welcome you. You are so happy to be back. However, it makes you sad to see the people standing around your body because they are crying. Moreover, it is a bit silly (so the guides say).

My hypnotherapist asked my guides if there is any way to offer comfort to the people who are sad after we die. The answer was that this is the point at which time is all warped. This is because in just a short period everyone around you will die too and they will be with you again. They just need to understand that you are not gone and they will see you again.

After we die, we do not go to a certain place. Rather, in soul form we are beams of light so we move around a lot and we go with the people we love, occasionally traveling to other planets. I think everybody has a home world. The Arcturians said that my home world is the Arcturian world. It has a lot of water and it is a beautiful green world. However, as a soul I can come back to earth and be with someone in just a moment's time.

When I asked the Arcturians about their sense of other worlds, they said they believe that there is an endless amount of other worlds. We only see a few stars and each star has so many planets. They are sending me messages all the time. They send everyone messages all the time. They say we need silence to feel them.

The best way to hear the messages is to find a peaceful place and get comfortable. Talk to The Lord. Go into a trance and talk to your guides and wait for your answers. They will be very happy and will answer any question you ask. They want to let us know that they love us very much, much more than we can imagine. We can just hang out in the cosmos and travel among the souls in the blink of an eye when we are in trance.

After spending time in lives between lives, we may decide to go to a planet and have a life experience. To do this we look for a mother who is pregnant and if we think we can help, we are drawn to her. Maybe it is someone we knew before. Our souls are attracted to pregnant mothers. Mothers are attracted to our souls, too.

The soul enters the body when the body is already formed (it is rather cramped). The entry may happen perhaps in the third trimester or end of the second trimester of pregnancy. However, when the soul enters the mother, the soul (you) are no longer connected to everything, but you become connected to your mother. Your spirit guides are with you, you just don't know it anymore. It is not that you forget; it is just not anything you think about as a fetus. (Please see chapter on Fear/Anxiety – Fear of Death)

Chapter 12

Depression

W ith all of my medical issues and life-threatening illnesses, I have never experienced pain as I have with depression. Depression should not be taken lightly.

Costada helped me get over my depression, just as your spirit guides will help with yours. As you speak to your guides about your feelings of depression, the overwhelming love you will draw from your guide will help to carry you through the pain you are experiencing. Feelings of sadness, fatigue or simply the lack of interest in doing something can all be attributed to depression. Your guides are always by your side. The power of their love as they try to help you is so pure that you will find yourself agreeing with their guidance and accepting it. Eventually you will feel strengthened again as you are lifted out of depression and feel your self-love grow and grow. It is difficult to be depressed when there is so much genuine love around you. When I asked my guides how to get over depression, they gave me a number of different techniques.

Technique 1

I was feeling depressed. A doctor said my blood was lacking certain necessary elements. He instructed me to take a vitamin B-12 pill, and my mood lifted the next day. The depression did return eventually, but having my mood lifted was a wonderful experience. I now take B-12 every day. It was a nice, quick fix, but only beneficial to people low in vitamin B-12.

Technique 2

Meditation/self-hypnosis is excellent for depression. This is because when you are in trance your brain waves are in theta, and through them one can feel connected to the universe. As you sense the spiritual love that is a dominant power of the universe, it is hard to stay depressed. Just ask your guides what they think about you. Their answer will be love. When you are loved so deeply, the depression lifts.

In trance, as in sleep, there is no depression. When I asked my guides how a person could get rid of depression, my five Arcturian guides came out in a semicircle in front of me. Before this they had always been behind and to the sides of me. Now I noticed they came to the front of me when I asked them questions on depression.

The Arcturians said that I would become depressed again. When that happens, I need to remember the depression will end. I am not going to miss the potential fun in my future. Always remember the temporary nature of depression. I tell myself that I know I am powerful and in control. I can control my thoughts and choose not to let depression in.

When asking the reason for my depression, I was told I was dwelling on sad events in my past. The Arcturians told me that I feel alone. While in trance, I am standing on the grass in a beautiful meadow in my mind. I see the past is the past. Only now matters. Our emotions should relate to the present. I can see that I am not alone, because I have The Lord and my guides with me at all times. We all do.

Technique 3

Please see Chapter on Self-Love – Body Image – Self-Worth. It is difficult to be depressed when you have such love from your guides, and since you love and respect them so, you come to realize that you too are great – and your self-love will blossom.

Technique 4

Another time I asked how depression could be overcome. I received three orbs to help deliver messages of healing and overcoming depression.

ORB 1

The first orb turned into a very close friend who broke my heart. I'd known her for a while, so I felt comfortable telling her I had cancer. Once she knew, she said not to call her anymore. I tried to call her, but she would not take my calls. I have hardly spoken with her in years. The Orb said this related to my depression because the person I had relied on told me she did not want me in her life.

How could I heal this painful relationship? Well, either I could put the relationship in my past or I could try to bring the relationship back in my life. As for how I could heal the relationship, I could go over the conversation until I reached as close to the truth as I could get. If I do not agree with what the person said that hurt me, I do not have to pay attention to what they said. If they say negative things, you can ignore them because it is not in your best interest to dwell on them. Remember, what people say usually says more about the speaker than the listener does.

We help people with depression in general with hypnotherapy. If a person is depressed they are probably reliving a negative event that happened in their past, when in reality there is no need to dwell on it. Know the past is in the past and that it has no control over you, unless you have a specific, positive reason for letting it.

The orb also said that people who are depressed can still have control over their thoughts. They should just have a good thought at the ready to focus on, or perhaps turn to an activity like reading or writing or meditating – anything to break the downward despairing cycle that occurs in our minds with depression.

It is not difficult to discover a happy thought. People should look back on their life to a happy or funny event. For instance, a happy memory could be their marriage ceremony, the birth of a child or hearing someone say I love you for the first time. Focus on the beautiful memory, and it will lighten your depression. It is very empowering for people when they realize they have control of their depression.

Lastly, the guides remind us to twirl a few times. It is hard to twirl and not smile.

Step by Step – How to Lift Depression

1. Identify what you were thinking about just before your feelings of depression set in. Ask yourself if there is any truth to them. If there are any negative comments within the framework of your thoughts that you disagree with, just toss them away outside your energy circle. You can also write them down and "physically" throw them away.

2. Then you must meditate and meet your spirit guides. I used to have a lot of self-loathing until I met my guides. With their love, I started seeing their point of view and for the first time I loved myself.

It is very hard to stay depressed when you truly love yourself. It will also be easier to love others more freely and genuinely. The depression will start to lift and you will think better of yourself, which is a natural reaction after self-hypnosis. It is also important to be aware of your thoughts. It takes practice, but you can stop yourself from focusing on the negative events that get you down. Consider it wasted energy.

ORB 2

The second orb that came to me had a little mirror in its face. I asked why the mirror was there and the orb told me that it was reflecting the truth back to me. You should look in the mirror, look yourself in the eye, and go over what is causing your depression. When you cry, look at yourself cry. Once you have done this, go into trance and ask your guides what it is that is making you depressed. They will give you the answer.

You will know the answer is coming from your guide because the answer will surprise you. Messages from our guides are different from the way our minds usually respond. Once they receive the answer, people will be able to perceive a better image of themselves because they will see themselves in the light of their guides' love. No matter what is wrong with you, know that your body and spirit are a gift from God and that he does not make mistakes. When people feel better, their bodies and souls reflect it.

Step by Step

1. Pinpoint what made you depressed.
2. Determine if there is there truth to it.
3. If there isn't any, just ignore it.
4. If there is truth - something you regret, just commit to not doing it again.
5. Ask the spirit guides and The Lord what they think of the person who caused you to become sad. People will feel overwhelming love from their guides that will be stronger than their depression. There are endless amounts of love, and love completely crowds out the depressive thoughts. If you are having difficulty with depression, use a trance

to welcome the abundance of love from your spirit guides and become cheerful again.

ORB 3

The last orb had a big knife in front of it. The orb said, "When we die, we go to heaven, the beautiful blue/white world, and we will be so thrilled to be back in our natural state. However, do not use the knife on yourself because the depression waxes and wanes. If you use the knife, you lose the good times too." The more you meditate, the more good periods you have.

Steps to relieve heavy depression

1. Do not forget, this will pass.
2. It will come back, but it will pass again.
3. Many people are depressed due to loneliness, but if they would spend time in trance with their guides, the depression would lift and they would know they are not alone.
4. God gave us depression to accompany periods of mourning, but he never intended for people to stay in a dark depressive state. Instead, people should meditate and bask in the loving light provided by their guides.
5. God welcomes you at all times, but he wants you to stay on this planet and work through your problems because it is the only time we can grow. We need bodies for that.
6. Do not suffer alone too much. You can always call a hotline and talk to someone about your troubles.

Chapter 13

Fear/Anxiety

There are probably as many fears as there are people. I need not list all the issues that frighten people. Simplistically, fear is concern about what might happen in the future.

Fear is the lowest emotion we can experience. Sometimes when I am very scared, I reach for the defensive feelings of anger since it is a higher, not as painful, emotion. Love is the highest emotion. Unless one is in imminent danger, most fear is based on concern over the future. We have no control over the future, so fear of it is a wasted emotion that does not allow you to enjoy the current moment.

Once when I asked what I was so afraid of, Costada told me, "You are not able to handle the truth." I loved this message. I felt like I was being watched over. Many months later, I was diagnosed with MS. Apparently, I had had it all along since I was a teen and diagnosed with epilepsy. At that stage, I viewed having MS as a terrible fate, even worse than cancer. It took time, but I overcame my fear and dislike of having MS; since then, I've learned how to make it better (please see Chapter on Neurological Issues).

Technique One - Fear of Death

When I asked about death, I was told that we are eternal. I am to remind people that we do not die. Most people do not know what will happen the moment after they die, thus they fear death. People are afraid of things they do not know. There is also the fear of being forgotten and dying alone.

No one should be afraid of death. It is simply a transition; it is like birth. The moment following death, we return home, back into the beautiful pure blue/white light existence of souls. Here you can be with any soul you want instantly. We are connected to all others in the cosmos, as well as to the group you have selected to travel with through time. Everyone is there. People are not in the same form but you will recognize them by their soul just as they recognize you. Once you go into a trance, you can talk to anyone. Once you die, you are again with everyone you ever knew. Later you can decide if you want to take another journey by way of a body.

Once you die, you can relax because you will know you are eternal. You will know that The Lord truly exists and that you will have knowledge about all your past lives in addition to knowing about all the souls you have ever met. You will also know you just died and can see your body resting in its last place on earth, wherever that may be. The process of physical death is slow and gentle, stopping one cell at a time.

One way to overcome fear of death is to do a past life regression. Then you will know that you have lived before, that reincarnation exists, and you will continue to live on eternally. At the end of doing a past life regression, go to the death scene and find out how and why you died. It will be very reassuring because you are alive now and you know you were alive previously so naturally and logically, you will be alive in the future.

When you are nearing death, and know there is life after death, you will know that it is time to go home. In addition, you will be happy about that, because you miss the strong connections with people you have when you are just a soul in lives between lives.

The guides like death because then you get to go back and play with other souls and guides who exist in their dimension. The journey we are on is infinite, just like our souls. It is important to get to know your guides in this life and to know that you are always connected to them. They do a lot to keep us on our path, and thanks to them, we usually end up with the people we are supposed to end up with in this life.

People should be aggressive in trying to overcome their fear of death. Fear is one of the harshest feelings the body can experience. You should love your body enough that you don't want to exist in an anxious state. The aim is to get to the root cause of the fear.

Technique Two – Past Life Regressions

I have always had an anxiety condition. When a friend asked me what I was so afraid of, I realized I had never thought of that. When I did, I realized I had a fear of being chased by jungle cats and having to run for my life.

On a separate, but related note, I used to wonder why cats and dogs fluff up their ruff of fur on their necks and cats fluff up their tails when they are in a flight-or-fight mode. It seemed foolish to me. I figured a lion's mane, for example, would hinder the lion in battle as some animal could grab all that hair.

I went to a hypnotherapist who told me to go back in time to the lifetime that is responsible for my conscious current fear of being attacked and feeling as if I have to run for my life. I went into trance and did a past life regression. I saw myself alone, very long ago. I was in an intensely vivid green valley and there was a huge cat with big teeth in front of me. I knew that I was going to be attacked. I remember lying on the ground with the cat above me. Using my hands, I grabbed the sides of the animal's mouth to keep him away from my throat. But all I could grasp was hair. I pushed his head away as much as I could, but the hair kept me from grabbing him. Then I died.

After this enlightening experience and living on the thirteenth floor in a building in Manhattan, I knew I had no reason to fear being eaten by a jungle cat. I was able to cut my anti-anxiety prescription from 14 pills a day to just 5 as the knowledge enabled me to rid myself of the fear, which was just a holdover from another lifetime.

When I meditated, my guides said that I feared dying because of the uncertainty of what would happen. It took a few years, but I overcame my fear of death since I now know that there is life after death. I continue to suffer from anxiety, but to a much lesser degree. I asked Costada why I have so much fear and lack of faith that others would come to my aid in an emergency. She told me to go back to an early trauma.

I remembered I had surgery and was hospitalized twice as an infant. Fifty-five years ago, they did not do much for children's pain, and I remember being behind the bars of the crib and I was crying and alone. Suddenly I felt a huge weight lifted from me. The awareness and recognition of the event, and, mainly, the knowledge that it happened over 50 years ago caused the anxiety to fade. I let the fear go, knowing I was now an adult capable of taking care of myself. I know I could trust my Lord, my guides, and my instincts to keep me safe.

Technique Three

One way to reduce fear is to go into a trance and imagine breathing all your fears, anxieties, and tension into a big, white bubble, in a manner similar to dealing with emotional pain. Search your entire body for hidden fears. Exhale them into the bubble. As more fears enter the bubble, it becomes larger and darker. When you have breathed out all the fears you could find, notice how large and dark the bubble has become. Then blow it away. Watch as it drifts away from you with each breath. Blow it over the horizon, where it explodes into nothingness producing a starburst effect. You will find old memories or fearful thoughts are no longer so bad. The past is in the past and has no hold on this moment.

Lack of confidence can lead to fear. Know that there is usually no need to be afraid. In addition, you know that if you find yourself in a scary situation, you have faith that you can get yourself out. This knowledge can be a confidence builder, because you know how to ground yourself this way at any time. This makes you less anxious since you know that you can solve the problem if you get nervous.

Costada's Technique - Overcoming fear with flowers

One way to overcome fear is to start with something that is not scary. Go into a trance. Imagine walking down a gorgeous footpath. You come to three flowers. Each one will give you a message regarding fear and how to overcome it.

I did this exercise, and the first flower I saw was a giant yellow tulip. It was as tall as I am. When I touched this flower, it revealed something I needed to see. When I touched it, it said "fear," reflecting the deep, dense, dark inside of the flower. It seems impossible to penetrate. However, with my guides beside me, I knew I would come out the other side of the flower and into the sunshine. From this, I learned that darkness does not mean danger and there is nothing frightening about the dark. Day follows night, so know the darkness is only temporary.

The second flower I saw was burgundy and unique. It was about four feet tall with many petals to remind me that I'm not alone – ever. When I touched the flower, it revealed to me I have a fear of water – mainly a fear of drowning. This is a holdover from a past life when I died in a tidal wave in Asia. That is why water comes up in my messages frequently. The guides are proud of me for living in a house with a stream on the property. It is helping me get over my fear of water.

The flower had a general message as well. If you look at an intimidating situation as if it were a game, you should explore every part of it. In other words, search out why you have this fear by going deep into every part of the flower (or fear). Again, with your guides beside you, you will find nothing to be afraid of and the fear will dissipate.

Look at your fear like a science experiment - you can dissect it, determine the cause and see if there is any truth to it and it won't be scary anymore. The next time you have the fear, you can just do the same thing. You can also pull off any petals you don't want and toss them away outside of your energy field. You can get rid of fear that way. I was afraid of my basement and attic. However, I explored them, and threw the fears away and now I am not afraid of them anymore.

The third flower I saw was purple and lavender, like a violet, and about five feet tall. It was shaped like lily of the valley and if I walked under it, I could put one on my head. Moreover, it smelled so good.

When I touched the flower, it told me that I have a fear of death. There are so many flowers on this stalk. My main fear is of dying alone. This is foolish because I am not going to die alone (I used to be afraid because the four times I was diagnosed as terminally ill, I was alone in a hospital). I now know my guides will be with me, so I (we) will not die alone.

The overall message is that you do not have to be afraid of death. You do not have to be afraid of being alone. Your guides are always by your side, even if you have never identified them. If you are afraid of dying, please do not be foolish and dwell on the subject, as you will miss the joy of the current moment.

There are simply two choices. Live in fear or live free of fear. Most of our fear is of what is going to happen in the future. Do not worry about the future; it will take care of itself and you have no control over it anyway.

We should go through our fears one by one. Explore them until they are irrelevant or until you are sick of reliving the worst-case scenario. Love and have faith in yourself and God; this goes a long way toward eliminating fears. Remember, love always triumphs over fear because there is so much more of it.

Chapter 14

Weight Loss – Food

When we exist in lives between lives and decide we want to have another in-body experience, we choose a family and a body we want. We pick our bodies. Each body has a certain weight. You have to find out what your natural weight is. Your body knows this already. To find out the correct body weight, go into a trance and bring in your guides. Ask them to show you your natural genuine body. They will explain that you chose this body and this family. The guides say we should love whatever weight it is.

I wanted to lose weight so I asked my guides how. They responded by asking why it was important. I found this very interesting, as they had never asked me a question before. I said it is important to lose weight because it affects how I feel about myself and physically everyone is healthier at an average weight. They agreed with the point that ideal weight helps you physically but otherwise weight is not important.

If you want to lose weight to get to your natural size, consider the following: Eating is a habit. Habits make life easier. The wonderful thing about habits is that they can be changed.

Start in the morning by eating less. Make a game out of it. The guides stress that making new eating habits must be fun; otherwise, you will not participate. Take your plate of food and eat exactly one-half of it. If you have to put the food into a little square shape and cut it in half, then do it. You can play with your food this way and you can take your weight down. It is important to start in the morning. Moreover, it is even more important to do it enjoyably. See if you can do it at exactly 50%. Drinking water is also very important.

Guides are very much into movement. They recommend taking a walk after every meal. Weight has nothing to do with your soul. Your soul is what is important and what you should be working on. Our bodies are just transient. Acceptance is also important. We should be in the habit of being very happy with what we have. People should not have unrealistic thoughts about how much weight to lose. They should get to the weight their guides tell them to be. Our guides love us the way we are. They are always sad when we are upset about our weight. That is something that should stop.

I asked what my genuine weight was. My guides think my weight is fine, but they are much more easygoing than we are. They don't know the difference between 20 and 30 pounds one way or the other. They believe thinking about how much you weigh is a waste of energy. They look at weight as money in the bank. If we find ourselves in a situation where there is no food, we will be able to survive longer if we have extra weight. On this planet most of the problems with food is that there is not enough of it.

Technique for losing more than 20 pounds

If you want to lose more than 20 pounds, and your guides think you should, increase your physical activity. Play and have fun. Do twirls, turn chores into playtime by dancing to music. Use your imagination to make it enjoyable.

You can go into trance and imagine what you looked like when you were happy with your weight. Be sure your guides agree that was a proper weight for you. Then imagine you and your guides have a large powerful magnet placed on the front of your body. This magnet can pull off the excess fat. You get to feel a little hungry. However, it becomes a habit as you get used to not feeling too full. Do not eat so little that you are weak and dizzy, just a little hungry. We have a tendency to eat until we are over full.

However, if you want to take weight down, pay attention and just eat half. Soon it will become a habit and weight will naturally fall off. Stop all extraneous eating and snacking. Do not eat food mindlessly and only eat what you need. The guides make it sound so simple, but to them it is not an issue. They say most people do not have enough nutritious food to eat. Being overweight is an issue for America, just not the planet.

Find a remedy for the underlying condition that food seems to help. This is the hard part: identifying what the underlying condition is. It could possibly relate to a very traumatic and negative childhood event. You will be able to remember when you are in trance. If you keep reliving the traumatic event, it will become irrelevant and will no longer have negative power over you. It will just be something in your distant past; stress how long ago it was and that you survived. The past is not important, only the present moment matters. You can let go of your past and any negative habits you have accumulated over your life.

How to determine if an item or food is good for you

This is one of my favorite exercises because it always works very well and it's fun. If you are not sure a food is good for you, have no fear. Your body knows. This requires two people, but no self-hypnosis. Hold your arm out in front of you. Have someone next to you try to push your arm down using only one finger. If you can hold your arm up, the second person should try to push down your arm with two fingers. If you can hold your arm up, the second person should then try with three fingers, or four fingers, until your arm can be pushed down.

Then pick up something with sugar in it, like a cookie, and hold it in your other hand. Then have the second person try to push your arm down again. You will be amazed at how difficult it is to hold up your arm up. It usually takes a few less fingers. This works because the sugar disrupts your energy field.

You can do this with any food. It differs for everyone. Yet it tells you what is good for your body and what should be avoided. The real key is to listen to your body, give it want it wants rather than what you are in the mood for. Listen to your cravings, unless they are for empty calories, like candy. I have been listening to my body crave ginger, cinnamon, red meat, spinach, flax seeds and black licorice. Subsequently I learned that all these cravings helped heal some of my various issues.

Chapter 15

Financial Health

When I asked Costada about wealth, she said it really doesn't have anything to do with money. It just concerns people's ideas about wealth. For instance, people can feel wealthy simply because there's a lot of love in their family despite the fact that they may not even have a change of clothes. Alternatively, consider that there are people who have millions of dollars and they are still unhappy.

There is so much more to being wealthy. With love and shelter and having people you want around you, you can be wealthy. There is so much more wealth than being just by yourself and having all the money you could want. You cannot buy people and you cannot buy their love. As long as we have enough money to buy food and shelter, everything else is just extra.

My guides reminded of a young girl I sponsor in Kenya. She is so proud of what she has. I sent her two pictures of my family and me and she just loves them. They make her feel wealthy. I find that the idea that merely two photographs could provide a feeling of wealth for someone is simply astounding and beautiful. She planted a banana seedling in my honor. That made me feel wealthy and humbled. The guides feel many of us have the wrong opinion of wealth. They think it is wrong to want more money. Mistakenly, people view it as something they want instead of realizing that they have wealth already.

The Arcturians are very much into playing. In addition, they encourage me to avoid doing things that do not please me. The one exception is work. Work has to be done, but the benefit is that you are paid. I love the Arcturians. They are into the big picture, but are still pragmatic.

PHYSICAL HEALING

Chapter 16

Neurological Issues – Multiple Sclerosis, Traumatic Brain Injury, RSD, Neuropathy (numbness) and Nerve Pain

Multiple Sclerosis

I had relapsing remitting Multiple Sclerosis for over 35 years. It then became progressive MS, and I became involved in holistic healing as an alternative to traditional medicine. The result: I got better. Odd for a progressive disease, but this is just another example of the wonders I have found with holistic healing.

The problem with MS is that it is an autoimmune disorder, where they body kills off the myelin sheath surrounding and protecting the nerve cells. Therefore, people with MS get clusters of dead cells in their brains and/or spines. However, I have additional neurological issues and have found the following advice from my guides to be phenomenal for neurological or nerve issues.

Homeopathy/Neuropathy

A number of years ago I met with Dr. Lawrence Galante, an accomplished homoeopath. With my MS came neuropathy, unsteadiness and the tendency to fall. Therefore, I walked with either a walker or cane for years, but I haven't had to use one since I met with Dr. Galante. He put me on a homeopathic medication. I started feeling the pain in my legs and feet again, as they had been numb for many years. I have been walking fine without a walker for the past four years. In addition, my falls are down from a couple a month to one or two a year. If I forget to take the pills for a few days, my legs become weak again. I can't stress how powerful a healing tool homeopathy can be.

How to create a healing substance with your guides ▨▨▨▨

During one hypnotherapy session, my guides put together a magical healing "spackle". I highly recommend that while in trance, you call in your spirit guides and have them stand in front of you. Imagine a table with a beautiful bowl placed in the center of it. Request that your guides add the ingredients that you need to make a magic healing spackle.

When I did a session on making a healing substance, my first Arcturian contributed a goopy substance similar to Vaseline to the bowl. Next, another Arcturian sprinkled sequins in the bowl. Arcturians have the ability to see the many different facets. A white healing powder followed into the mix. The next Arcturian put in a burst of light since that is what usually heals me. John put in his magical feathers. Lastly, Costada put her hands in the mixture, stirred it, energized it and infused it with healing love.

This is what came next and you can do this too. While in a trance, take a tiny magic brush and some spackle and brush it over the area that hurts. This should cause the pain to subside. Then imagine following the painful area's nerves up to where they reside in your brain (unless the pain is completely localized pain). Part of your brain will be a little painful. Take the brush and coat the area of your brain that is attached to your pain. Paint the spackle along each nerve cell. This will help heal the nerves in your brain and those at the area of discomfort.

I have found this to be an excellent healing exercise that I use for many of my various neurological problems, mostly because of my multiple sclerosis. However, I have found it useful on all pain.

Nerve Pain

If you have a painful area, find the area that hurts and highlight the area in your brain that is connected to your place of discomfort. Once you have identified the area in your brain, ask this area of pain what it wants.

My brain wanted attention and wanted to be healed. I asked about what form of attention, and it simply wanted acknowledgement that it hurt. My guides suggested putting some white spackle on the hurtful area with a small magic brush. As I applied the spackle, the pain started to dissipate. You can also do this exercise in your awake state, once you find that particular place in your brain that hurts, and you can continue to work on it. However, I have found it most beneficial to practice while in a trance.

Remember the problem is not always with the specific area that hurts, it can be coming from nerves. My guides say that nerves love nothing as much as healing energy flowing up and down them. That is their reason for existing. Feel the energy in the Chi as it flows up and down your body. Revel in it.

Notice what color the energy is. For me it was red. I found this a very comfortable color because the inside of me is red so it feels like home. Allow the particles of light to spread out. All the nerves want is to be used. In addition, they want to help each other. When you give your nerves the attention notice how the pain lessens and goes away. I also use green light if I have an area of pain, although I have worked with all colors.

For me, I focused on fixing the pain in my head connected to the bone tumor in my hand, wrist, arm and elbow. My arm felt all better. I told the cancer to grow more slowly. It told me it wanted a Lidoderm patch, which took away all the pain (even though the doctor said it would not help).

Technique 1 – Nerve Pain

As mentioned, we can have painful areas that originate from our brain or spine. Interestingly, I have found that if I have a painful area of my body, and I focus on it in trance, I can follow the nerve up to where the pain is in my brain or spine. This is very useful to know, as not all pain is localized.

Highlight the brain area connected to your area of discomfort. Isolate that area by putting a bubble or cloud around it. You can do this in your awake state. Keep on working on the area. Do not be surprised if the problem area moves around throughout your brain. Just keep working on it. Use the magic spackle, and go about healing cells in a burst of light or gently stretching the nerves so they work better at the ends.

Remember, a pain in your leg or foot, for example, doesn't necessarily start there, it could emanate from the nerves – possibly your brain and/or spine. Nerves love all the attention you can give them. What I have found to be very healing is to imagine the light moving around my body. It moves faster and faster. It loves the energy going up and down inside you. Some may say the chi is flowing freely.

In this meditation, I received the message that nerves just want to be used. They all want to help each other. I concentrated on the nerves in my legs and back and I no longer had pain in my feet where I have a nasty, painful neurological condition, called RSD (reflex sympathetic dystrophy).

(Please see chapter on Back Pain – Little workers – nervous system specialists for another way to help heal nerve pain.)

Chapter 17

Dystrophy

I have reflex sympathetic dystrophy (RSD). This means that my sympathetic reflex nerve that goes down both legs is shrinking. This is because I fell and I stayed on the floor, crushing my ankle and cutting off the blood supply to my foot for about 10 minutes (read this to mean if you ever fall, don't lie there and cut off the blood flow to any area). When I cut off the blood supply to my foot, it caused my sympathetic nerve to start to die. I do not have muscular dystrophy and have no advice on how to deal with such a condition. I do know, however, how to deal with dystrophy of a part of your body.

I have dystrophic nail beds; my toenails kept falling off and did not regrow, due to the RSD. This condition caused me terrible pain in my toes, as the nerves started to shrink/die. I was told this was a progressive disease. Again, contradicting medical knowledge, in six months of working on them weekly in trance, the nail dystrophy is healing and my nails are growing back.

I found out that the tips of my toes that hurt are connected to an area in the left side of my brain that is behind my eye. I can feel the energy, the Chi, going up and down very fast between my brain and my toes. It is very healing. The energy is a beautiful gentle wash of color up and down my body problem. My guides really like the movement of the blue light going back and forth to my brain. Sometimes the body just needs to reconnect to itself.

Costada told me that the activity in my toes is getting better. The guides just want me to go into trance and keep mentally rubbing down my legs and my feet pulling down the nerves. They also want me to be very gentle to the nails and the tips of my toes. I should put cream on my hands and rub it into my feet. Pay attention to the little toe tips.

If you have similar pain, take the advice of my podiatrist, Dr. Philip Whitman, DPM. He instructed me to buy shoes one size larger so my toes wouldn't touch the front of my shoes and hurt. This was such a wonderful and simple solution to a terrible problem. If you think your feet look too big in bigger shoes, after a day of no foot pain they will look lovely to you.

Chapter 18

Reiki

R eiki is a healing technique using hands to channel energy through touch. It was developed in Japan by Mikao Usui in the early 20th century as a form of spiritual medicine. Hands are placed directly on the body or just above the skin, but in the energy field. When you have an open mind, you can connect with the healing energy of the Reiki practitioner whose aim is to promote and restore your well-being.

Reiki, according to Costada, is very good around the head and face. The guides are very receptive to healing energy and participate in the Reiki process by giving us messages – it is part of our guides' essence. When employing the Reiki technique, the guides are there to monitor the energy transferred and brought through your body by the practitioner's hands. Their own guides are able to give them messages concerning the best treatment for you. As a result, you will tingle with your own guide's love as you in turn receive their messages.

As hands move down the body and the tingling increases, the loving energy of the universe is drunk in - as you work down the body, feel the energy go around you in a circle and let it heal anything that needs healing. Keep your mind open and feel how much power there is from the hands. As they tap into the powers of the cosmos they have an endless amount of strength. The body will feel the beautiful love and energy.

The Arcturians prefer Reiki when hands are on the body rather than just above the body, but I have found it to work both ways. The Reiki practitioner will be able to tell which parts of a person's body needs more attention. Reiki masters are also a conduit for the elimination of bad emotions and pain.

Chapter 19

Cancer – Chemotherapy and Healing a Cancerous Tumor

M y first diagnosis of terminal cancer (metastasized squamous cell cancer of unknown primary) gave me 12-24 months to live. Costada, however, told me that I would not die young. I had lived those years already. I was 46 at the time and found the comment shocking and insulting but true.

After performing a major surgery, the doctors on staff at one hospital (Memorial Sloan Kettering Cancer Center) did not want me to do chemotherapy or radiation, suggesting instead that I just enjoy the months I had left. Luckily, doctors at New York Presbyterian Hospital felt it was worthwhile to treat me with radiation and chemotherapy. That was over 10 years ago.

When I was first diagnosed with terminal cancer, I started to see a healer. I worked with healer-hypnotist Mr. Ron Navarre who has developed wonderful healing practices for cancer patients involving breathing and teaching patients how to find healing energy within themselves. He puts patients into a trance and then tapes the session so they can meditate while listening to the tapes during chemo infusions. You can imagine how stressful cancer treatments are and I have used this approach when dealing with clients who have cancer, with excellent results.

I recommend looking at *The Hidden Messages in Water* by Masaru Emoto. In it, the author tells how he would fill a beaker of water. A sign would be placed before the beaker. The sign would say joy, for example. Then young Buddhist school children, would pray for the water to feel joy. Then they would freeze the beaker of water, take a slice of the frozen water, and look at the crystals that formed. It was amazing how beautiful love crystals are. The most stunning crystals were for knowledge while the worst came from polluted water.

I incorporated this exercise into my chemotherapy sessions. When the chemo was about to begin I'd place my hands on the outside of the chemo bag and say all positive words – love, peace, health, joy, bliss, knowledge, and happiness – to infuse the chemo with positive energy. Just as the Buddhist school children did. So only positives, not poison, entered my body.

After I infused the water, I would put on the chemo meditation recording and go into trance. My advice is to find a beautiful place in your mind where you can relax. Remember Pac-Man? Imagine a little army of Pac-Man figures or robots contained in the chemotherapy fluid. As you welcome this magical army into your body, direct the fluid to your cancer area. Find a cancer cell, and have one of the Pac-Man figures or robots surround the cell. Then imagine they squeeze or chomp on the cancer cell. Suddenly in a burst of light, the cancer cell is gone, and a new healthy cell replaces it. One after another, find and remove the cancer cells.

It is extremely important to have the correct attitude to heal cancer. This is difficult but vital if you want to survive. When I first meditated on my cancer, I said I hated it. Costada said it was a part of me. How can I hate part of me? The cancer is just damaged cells that are growing too fast. I saw that if I truly loved myself I needed to accept all of me – cancer included. Once I no longer was fighting an enemy but rather bringing love of self to include the damaged cancer cells, my health and mood improved drastically.

My guides suggested switching places with the cancer. This is easily done while in trance. Take the cancer and place it on a chair in front of you and then ask it questions. I asked the cancer what its personality was like. It replied, "I am tough squamous cells. I've given you extra for you to see that strength is not a good thing. Fighting cancer cells is wrong. Accept them with love, and accept that part of yourself." My cancer is here, like my other ailments. Being strong is not this life's objective. It was in a past, unhappy life. I need to break free of thinking strength is beneficial and necessary for life. Life will take care of itself.

I went into remission after one treatment of chemo even though the doctors said it didn't work that way and I still needed six more months of treatment. My dermatologist wrote a paper on me because I was on two strong drugs (Carboplatin and Paclitaxel) and didn't lose any hair. I suffered no ill effects from six months of chemotherapy.

A few years later, I was diagnosed with metastasized non-Hodgkin's lymphoma with tumors in my neck and hip. Unlike my prior cancer, this time I felt I only had a few months to live. Like the prior cancer, I had six months of strong chemotherapy. I meditated during the first treatment, using the little Pac-Man robots to take away the cancer cells. I went into remission. Again, I amazed my doctors. I spent the next five months very depressed so I did not meditate during the treatments, and they were so difficult. I had so many negative side effects. I also lost all my hair. The difference, I know, was the meditation.

Healing a cancerous tumor

I have pain in my left arm, wrist, elbow and hand from a very rare bone tumor (Melorheostosis). I am the 303rd person in recorded history to have such a tumor, and the second person to have it metastasized (into my leg).

If you have something you would like to get rid of, begin by focusing on the tumor/or issue that hurts. My guides say that my body needs the tumor I have to shrink. When I first started to work on the tumor in trance, it stopped hurting and the pain in my elbow disappeared.

In trance, I asked about the tumor and I received the message that the tumor is happy, and just continues to grow. This is not what I wanted to hear. I told the tumor to stop growing because the cells were damaged, and they were growing too fast. They were sick cells and they should easily leave my body. The tumor should not grow because it gives me pain.

I just had to give it attention. I needed to focus on healthy cells and have them overtake the bad cells. It is not a fight that is going on; it is more of a joining. If you have such an experience with cancer, you should ask the healthy cells to stay with you rather than join the tumor. Ask the healthy cells to take over the cancerous cells, and in a little burst of light the bad cells should disappear.

When I asked what the tumor wanted to say to me, it was that the tumor should leave my body because if it went into my bloodstream it would metastasize to other areas of my body. I could get the tumor to leave my body by chipping off little pieces of it with the blue light on the tips of my fingers. Again, if you have this experience, like droplets of water, the blue light washes over the tumor and happily cancerous cells drip from your fingers.

Water therapy is very good for eliminating tumors. In a shower or pool, keep rubbing that part of your body with the tumor and gently rub it down to the tips of your fingers or the tips of your toes. The cells will follow down and leave your body. Be sure to thank the tumor for the awareness that it gave you, release it with love, and let it go. It does not need to stay anymore.

I use this technique, but of all the exercises in this book, this one was the least effective. However, it does improve my pain, and bone cancer is considered the most painful cancer.

Technique Number 1

This technique can be applied to all cancerous tumors. First, while in trance, focus on the part of your body that has cancer. Imagine a red healing light encircling the hurtful area. The red light brings in blood, the ultimate healer. Feel the warmth. Then imagine the extra cancer cells just die and are carried safely away from your body through your bloodstream. Like our physical pain, what the area needs most is attention. Find out which color light is the best to help you heal your cancer. Experiment while in trance trying out various colors of light.

For me, red light helps to shrink my tumors. Whenever I have an area that hurts or is cold, I put a red warm healing cloud around it and it feels better. We (our bodies) know which cells are healthy and which are cancerous. Cancer cells grow faster. That is why you can sense your cancer.

The cloud technique is good for pain anywhere. Each wounded person or body area should find its own healing color. This is not difficult. The correct color will come in, just take note of it.

People think so much about getting better, but fail to put forth the effort to get better. Many people with emotional problems think about seeing a psychiatrist. While this is an excellent notion, people should remember to pay attention not only to their brain but also to their body. If your body is ill, it affects your brain. Luckily, your brain, body and guides can heal most illnesses, injuries or emotional issues.

To be cancer-free perform daily body scans. Bring in a healing color through your head, touching everything as it travels to your toes. Go through your body and find all the cancer. Pay attention to everything. Use guided imagery of Pac-Man or little robots to heal the cancer cells. Bring in the power of a healing light. You pick the color that feels best. The light is derived from the power outside. It's all love. Bring it into the cell until it explodes into a small starburst and a new healthy cell appears. Once the cell heals and touches another, the healing becomes contagious.

Chapter 20

Lymphedema

I have had over 20 lymph nodes, the lymphatic system and the surrounding tissue in my pelvis removed during cancer surgery. Yet I have no noticeable lymphedema. This is a condition that cancer patients suffer after lymph nodes are removed and the limb swells. Left alone, one can get elephantiasis (enlargement of a limb due to obstruction of the lymphatic muscles). It's best not to get lymphedema in the first place. To prevent lymphedema, you should you keep your limb in a compression garment. It is very important to see a lymphedema expert before your cancer surgery so you will know how to treat the limb right after the operation.

I saw someone before my surgery, and she had me in a compression garment when I was still in the hospital. I wear a stocking during the day and a large soft compression garment at night.

Treating lymphedema requires a qualified nurse to wrap your limb in low elastic bandages. This pushes the lymph fluid into your bloodstream where it leaves your body. I had my leg wrapped most days for the first year and twice a week after that. Eight years after the cancer surgery, doctors performed a test on me to see how the area where the lymph channels that were removed were performing.

These doctors were at the cutting edge of lymphedema. They were transplanting healthy lymph nodes into the area where the nodes had been removed after cancer. These doctors were simply amazed when they found I had regrown new lymphatic channels. The doctors did not know the body could do it. I was the first patient they had seen who had regrown lymphatic channels, further proof that we can heal ourselves. If you have lymphedema, do not worry over it. Just welcome it into your life and manage the condition with lymphedema wraps and compression garments. It need not be a painful, annoying condition. Give it the loving attention it wants and keep it in a compression garment, especially when you fly.

Unfortunately, I have found that cancer surgeons are not that concerned with lymphedema as they are with a reaction to the cancer surgery and lymph node dissection. Many will tell you that if you get lymphedema, you should just elevate the limb above your heart. I have not found this to be a worthwhile exercise because the lymph fluid would just travel up my leg and pool in my buttocks. As soon as I stood up, the fluid slowly started traveling back down my leg. So be proactive with your lymphedema.

Chapter 21

Pain

The most important way to alleviate pain is to listen to your body. Pain is simply an indicator; your body is sending you a message that it needs attention. Do not ignore pain, but don't wallow in it either. Instead, give the painful area the attention it craves.

Healing Technique Number 1

Some of my guide's responses are so simple, yet so powerful. When an area hurts, is diseased or injured, it needs one thing – attention. During a body scan, I received a message that I had forgotten my left leg, so it no longer felt like a part of me. That is because I had cancer and have no lymph nodes for that leg. I put my leg in a compression garment and then forgot about it for 10 years. Now that leg needs extra attention. Its needs loving. I take care of the right leg, I just forget about the left one. It wants cream gently rubbed in with a loving touch. It wants stretching. Make sure there is no part of your body you have forgotten about.

Healing Technique Number 2

I use this excellent healing exercise for many of my various neurological problems, mostly due to my multiple sclerosis. However, I have found it useful on all pain (please see Chapter on Neurological Issues, and making a healing substance with your guides).

Next, while still in a trance, take a tiny magic brush and some magic healing spackle your guides put together for you and brush it over the area that hurts. This will cause the pain to subside. Then imagine following the painful area's nerves up to where it resides in your brain (unless it is a completely localized pain). Part of your brain will be a little painful. Take the brush and coat the area of your brain that is attached to your pain with the magical spackle. Go along each nerve cell. This will help heal the nerves in your brain and at the area of discomfort.

Healing Technique Number 3

Technique Number 3 is an excellent healing method to eliminate pain in your back and neck, as well as the areas that hurt from referred pain. Start at the very base of your spine. Imagine you can see each vertebra. Slowly go up all 33 vertebrae of your spine. When you get to an area that hurts, coat it with the magic spackle. Notice any pain in your back radiating to a different part of your body. Gently paint the nerve fiber from your back with your little brush to the areas that hurt.

Healing Technique Number 4

It is important to have one fallback method for relieving pain. This is mine: If you ever have bad pain, ask your guides to put their hands on the painful area and the pain will dissipate. You can feel the warmth from their hand and it relaxes tight muscles and heals illness. Just relax into their hand, feel the warm power flow into you, healing all the damaged cells. The warmth of their hand will relieve muscle spasms. Feel the love and power in their touch.

Healing Technique Number 5

When you are in trance, imagine bringing blood to the area of your body that is in pain. In your mind, focus on the area as it gets all warm and red from the inflow of blood. Imagine the blood flowing and removing all the bad energy in the area that is painful. Feel the warmth of the blood. Focus on one cell in the area of discomfort. In a burst of light make the bad cell disappear. In its place you will find a brand-new healthy cell. This healthy cell will then touch the cell next to it and it will take on the healing properties as well. Soon your whole body feels so much better.

Healing Technique Number 6

Decide if you want to take the pain and surround it with a halo. Bring the pain into your body, absorb it and let it dissipate. I dealt with the pain from my bone tumors this way. I took the pain, smoothed it out along the bone, and it ceased to hurt. I have also lessened my back pain this way. Just allow the muscles to relax and stretch. Imagine that you have a little red cloud surrounding the area of discomfort. Feel the healing warmth of the cloud, as it brings blood to the painful area.

Healing Technique Number 7

The infinity sign (an eight on its side) is the universal reset symbol. Standing with your feet shoulder length apart make the sign of infinity with your hands very gently and very slowly. It should feel good. Then pick one cell in your body that is damaged. Make the infinity sign inside that cell. When you do this, the cell will become a wonderful healthy cell. When you make the infinity sign say to yourself that you want to be whole and healthy. The healthy cells are contagious, soon all the cells surrounding it become healthy as well. In just a moment, your whole body can heal this way.

Healing Technique Number 8

This technique applies to most pain that you have: back pain, knee pain, arm pain – pretty much any pain that troubles you. I have pain on the lower right hand side of my back. I usually have a large knot in the area. In trance, I was told to take a little ball of blue light and highlight the part of my back that hurts. Then take the blue ball that hurts and place it in a chair in front of you.

Ask:

- Why does this area hurt?
- What message does this area have for you?
- What is the personality of this pain?
- What does this area need to feel better?
- What can you do to make this area better?
- Why is this area telling you this today?
- What lesson can learned from this pain?

The more questions you ask the more information you receive. Moreover, the guides just keep giving answers for as long as you ask questions. They do not repeat themselves. That is why in this book there can be a multitude of healing techniques to solve one problem. This shows I asked it a question at least as many times as I received specific healing techniques.

When I did the exercise above, my answer was that I was crooked. I am just not properly aligned. I need to focus on my posture. When I go for an x-ray and lie down on the table, the technician always shifts my hips to line me up straight. It feels strange for me to be in that straight a position.

I had my spirit guides help me move and shift my hips while I was lying down in trance. The first time I shifted my hips I screamed out in pain. However, the second time I shifted my hips, again asking my spirit guides to help me, I had no pain. My back did not hurt. I need to find that straight position while I am not in a trance. However, I found to be it surprisingly difficult.

I never knew why I had that pain for so many years. I committed to allowing my body to align naturally. The key to it was discovering that I was not lying straight. I trusted my guides to find the aligned position and allowed them to shift my body. I was also told I needed to overcome my hip pain that had prevented me sleeping any way but on my right side for over 10 years. I was to sleep on my left side and put a pillow under my knee. Away went my hip pain.

If you need to be properly aligned, allow your guides to shift your body in the bed. Imagine and envision the flow of the energy from this aligned position. With each breath, the energy flow goes up and down. It is a wonderful feeling and a gift to your body. Always let the Chi flow.

The pain served its purpose in showing me why I had the pain and how to fix it. Reassure the pain that it did its job very well. Thank your area of pain and your guides for such a relief of pain. The lesson is the pain needs to be heard, which is why putting it on a chair in front of you works so well.

Stomach Pain

Another common complaint is digestive problems. I suffer every morning because I take a handful of pills on an empty stomach. Costada said I needed to coat my stomach before I put anything in it. This can be accomplished by eating or drinking a glass of milk before I take my pills. Although I had been told before about this, I didn't do it because a glass of milk is not appealing to me. My guides said that I was being stubborn. They say I cannot take pills on an empty stomach because it just eats holes in my stomach and that is why the pain ensues. If you have digestive problems, ask your gut what it wants to feel better. Then do it.

Chapter 22

Back Pain

L ike 80% of Americans, I have back pain. It is one of the main culprits in this country of people having to adjust their normal routine; for instance, back pain causes the inability to walk upright or sit in a chair and often results in a person missing work. I have had seven herniated discs and four spinal surgeries, including two fusions of four levels. In addition, the last fusion failed. I also have spinal stenosis and my vertebrae are no longer neatly lined up on top of each other (Retrolisthesis).

Technique 1 – Costada's Technique of Using Little Workers

When I asked how to heal my back, I was shown pictures of my brain and spine. There were white dots or lesions (caused by the MS) scattered throughout them. When I asked what my back wanted, attention was the answer, along with more of the magical white healing spackle.

My back had asked for spackle before, and I have always applied the spackle with what I call a magic-like brush. Recently, I was given a team of workers – little tiny men in overalls and construction boots who were very strong and stocky – and at the most only a quarter inch tall. They reminded me of Snow White's Seven Dwarfs. They started out by just walking all over my brain. Where needed, they applied spackle. They took their job very seriously. There was no general contractor; they were all equal. They navigated the crevices of my hypothalamus and cerebellum in search of white spots. When they found one, they grabbed hold of it and squeezed it with love. In a burst of light, they made it disappear with only healthy brain tissue remaining.

Next, they started walking single file down my spine. Again, when they came to a white lesion, they put their arms and legs around it, and squeezed it with love until it disappeared. I didn't need to tell them where it hurt. They knew instinctively where the problem was. They came to a large white lesion in my back. A number of the little workers put their arms around each other's shoulders and squeezed the white lesion into nothingness.

The handymen, as I call them, then just stomped up and down my spine taking away anything that did not need to be there and began softening up the tissue. Next, they very gently started rubbing the nerves that were signaling the pain, almost like a pat on the back. The nerves became calm and went out to heal the rest of my body.

The little workers have a specialty that can be adjusted depending on your need. They use different healing methods for different people. However, for me, they work mostly in my spine and brain because of my MS. After the workers finished stomping on the white lesions, my back felt so much better. They did not need to go to other parts of my body because they can heal my body by working on my brain and my spine. They are my nervous systems specialists.

Everybody has these little workers. They are the workers of the spirit guides and have been with me all along. They are very happy when you call them up to help solve a physical problem. It is good to bring them in after you have done a body scan so that they can heal the areas highlighted during the scan.

Suggestions from Guides for Back Pain

Go into a trance and perform a body scan. Focus on your brain and note any areas bothering you. Do the same for your spine and find areas that want attention. Try to connect the painful part of your back to the corresponding part in your brain or spine.

Call in your little workers as mentioned above. Notice what they look like. They can tell you what needs to be done and you can talk back. They will work on your brain and then your spine, making you feel good with all that attention.

Next focus on your back, outside of your spine, and find any areas that hurt. Much back pain is due to muscle spasms resulting from a structural problem. The handymen can work on nerve pain and muscle spasms, stomping out pain and softening the tissue. It is like getting a massage from the inside.

Next, bring in your spirit guides and all the little workers. Put the workers on a table, because they are so small. Notice how they are interconnected. When I asked Costada what she thought of the little workers she said she loves them. They are just little extensions of her. Everybody is such a different size. The Arcturians are so tall; Costada is almost my height and the little workers are 1/4″ tall. Costada says we can have as many workers as we want. John (my red-tailed hawk animal spirit guide) says he is bigger and more powerful than the workers are. He likes to be the head honcho!

Technique 2 – Heat

There is nothing new to putting heat on a painful back. When you are in a trance, go to your beautiful island. The air and sun are the perfect temperature. Feel the weightlessness of the magical place. It is as if you are in the water and do not have any pressure on your back.

Your back likes you to spend more time in warm water and on warm sand. You can bring the outdoor heat inside by employing heat sources, such as heating pads and heat wraps. I can also use the Arcturians. Their hands are so warm and large that when they touch my back, they just take the pain away. I love relaxing into their hands. The feeling of weightlessness continues.

The guides also say it is good to run warm water on your back in the shower. When you are in a trance, it is also good to imagine warm water running down your back. You can also bring in a red warm healing cloud. Have the little red cloud encircle your back and stomach. Feel the warmth of the cloud. Feel it permeate your skin and muscles and relax them.

The back also needs nourishment. The guides say we need lots of water (I prefer Double Helix water) and protein. They say our bodies need more meat and fruit.

When I asked my guides what to do for my back, I was told to get a massage, take hot baths, use a heating pad in bed, wear a heating wrap during the day, put on a Lidoderm patch, relax my back in a body scan and have perfect posture. I should keep giving it attention and it will heal itself. Pain is your body trying to get your attention. It is rude to ignore something that wants your attention. I have listened to my guides and my back pain is down over 90%.

Technique 3 - Exercise and Stretching

I know it can be tricky to exercise if you have a bad back, because you do not want to injury yourself. Nonetheless, listen to your back and move it. Staying in bed (for more than a few days) and not walking around will make your back worse.

Guides love us to stretch our backs. People with bad backs should just hang over until they can touch the floor again. Do not push yourself, do it very gently and with love for your back. Let gravity do all the work. If you try every morning, in a couple of months you should be able to touch the floor. Visualize yourself bending even further with each breath. For decades, I could not bend my back, but I can now touch the floor easily without pain.

Technique 4 – Acupressure

This exercise does not require you to go into a trance. You can do acupressure on yourself. This is also called pressure point massage. This is the only technique in this book that will give you pain. However, you will find it worth it, given how pain free you will be afterward.

First, feel around your back for the spot or spots that hurt the most when you press on them. Then remember where they are. Next lie down on a bed and make a knuckle with a finger. Take that knuckle and place it under the painful area of your back. Then just relax, lie back and let your body weight push you into the knuckle. This will hurt. Badly. However, let it work its magic. In a couple of minutes, the muscle spasm will release and the hard knot will be all soft. Then move your knuckle to another painful place, and repeat.

The Arcturians recommend massage for those in pain. If it is too expensive, they recommend that two friends give each other a massage. It is a perfect way to show yourself and a friend some love and attention.

Technique 5 - Place it on a Chair

As discussed in the Pain Chapter, go into a meditative trance. Using your inner eye, look at the inside of yourself and the hurtful area. Place the painful area in a bubble (for me it was a muscle spasm in my lower back) and put it on a chair facing you. Look and see if there is anything wrong with it. Ask it what it needs to feel better. Keep asking questions and more answers will come. For example: What is the message from this pain? What does it do for you? What is its personality? Why are your guides showing you this today?

Correct Posture to Alleviate Back Pain

When I learned how to stand straight, my back pain of 40 years vanished. I now stand with proper posture to keep the pain at bay. To stand straight, stand with your feet shoulder width apart. Look front. Rock forward gently to your toes and then rock to your heels five times. Then rock a little less five times, then with very little rocking and then stop. You will find perfect posture and the ability to stand straight without effort.

Maintaining Correct Posture to Alleviate Back Pain – Most Effective Exercise

I have a wonderful physical trainer, Mr. Tomas Hajek. My posture was poor and my balance was a challenge. He taught me the best physical exercise in this book. Consider an imaginary hook attached to your collarbone affixed with a string that stretches upward to the ceiling or sky. It is unbreakable and holds your body up straight. Imagine it, feel it and walk with the confidence of it. It will keep you walking upright, help with your balance and do wonders for your posture. After all, as Mr. Hajek says, if you walk hunched over, you are halfway into a fall. No matter which position you are in, always hold yourself up by your hooks. I do that every day and quite a few people commented on how great I looked and how much taller I appeared. This is so simple, but powerful, and it changed my life. It got rid of my chronic back pain and I no longer need to wear a back brace, which a doctor said I would have to do for life.

Emotional Freedom Technique

Lastly, I saw a tapping expert (emotional freedom technique). She had me go back to an early horrid trauma I had completely forgotten about. The tapping expert showed me how to tap on the meridian lines and repeat the fact that the event occurred over 50 years ago. Within moments, my back pain vanished. When it comes back, I repeat the exercise. I have found the key to tapping is finding the correct bad childhood memory and emphasizing how many years it has been since the event, so your body knows it is no longer in danger.

Chapter 23

Stability – Physical

S tability is one of my favorite topics. During one session, my hypnotherapist and I just could not think of a healing topic. I went into a trance and asked my guides to suggest one, and they chose stability. Stability, it turns out, is quite important. It is important to everyone, but particularly to me because I have a tendency to fall due to muscle weakness and balance problems resulting from having MS.

Physical Stability

Physical stability is vital, as a bad fall can leave you with a painful injury for years. Therefore, the guides are very interested in our physical fitness with the objective of improving balance and strength. If you live a sedentary life and are just beginning to exercise, know that our guides want us to get our bodies moving! Know your limits and start slowly. For instance, using two- or five-pound dumbbells are a good start and stay away from lifting extreme weights. Also, think of how animals play, stretch and stay active. Use the body that The Lord lent you, gently but constantly, except when you decide to rest.

Make becoming more active into a game. The guides are into playtime. It's as if when we become more advanced, play becomes more important. If it's not fun, why would you do it again? Find some movements that you will enjoy. Don't forget to add music which is always good for the body and spirit. Listening to the vibes of upbeat music can help us move more and have fun. Unfortunately, a variety of health conditions can affect one's stability. Exercise can help bring you to a more healthy physical being as you gain strength with every move.

You can make movement fun by imagining you are inside an amazing body that can move in so many ways. The guides want people to do a lot of stretching, but only if it is fun. As we enjoy standing and stretching more, our posture improves. Costada wants me to learn how often to stretch by emulating my cat, who is always stretching.

Breathing is a major factor in exercise. It enhances your concentration and keeps you in communication with your body. Focus on breathing as you move. Do all the movements with love. If you are sore after a workout, rub your aching body parts as a reward.

The message in movement and stretching relates to a way that you can love yourself. As humans, we are meant to stand on our own two feet, balanced and upright. Falling for any reason and injuring ourselves is a fact of life, but for some more so than others. Thus, we should be proactive and do all we can to prevent ourselves from this happening, particularly if we are prone to it. I have MS and have fallen over 100 times. However, I don't fall anymore. I now practice mindfulness living. More importantly, I take a remedy for neuropathy recommended by my homeopath. It allows me to feel my legs and the ground under my feet, and it most important - keeps me from falling. Many people lose their balance as they age. The guides recommend working out with a trainer, taking an exercise class and seeing a homeopath for a solution.

I asked my guides how to have physical stability. According to my guide, I just have to visualize looking down my path. It is straightforward. Just follow it. Everything we need for physical stability is within our circle. Everything on earth helps our stability; and the ground is flat and soft. Know that your hooks and your spirit guides are always with you holding you up. In addition, if you do fall, do not ignore it. Never ignore pain. If something is bothering you, show it some loving attention.

Chapter 24

Stretching and Movement

Stretching

Costada is very clear about our bodies. She says that they are a wonderful gift lent to us by The Lord, and we should love them and treat them with respect. The guides encourage us to stretch our bodies and to use them the way they were meant to be used. That entails gentle, frequent movements, like going for a long stroll rather than sitting all day. However, it does not include extreme sports. Stretching usually makes us feel good and while doing so, it is important for our well-being to be mindful of our breathing, body, spirit and mind. Below are included some stretching exercises and positions that I believe are necessary for us to take care of our total self.

We must work on staying fit without losing flexibility. Stretching should be fun. You can do stretches standing, sitting and lying down. All muscles are meant to be long and smooth. Watch the animals; they stretch constantly. Breathing is also a factor. Make your breathing part of the exercise. Do all the stretches with love. When you finish stretching, you can give some loving attention to the part of the body you had been working on.

Position 1 - Standing

When I begin stretching, I stand up with my palms together above my head like I'm praying, you can do the same. Take your hands and bring them down your center. Look at your hands and as they move downward, bend over and follow your hands down. Next, bend over, with your hands on the floor. Do the stretch even if you have to bend your knees. Then gently rise and bringing up the power of mother earth, as you raise your hands to your sides and up above your head, welcoming in the powers of the heavens. Then bring your hands back down. Keep repeating the movement. Move gently and slowly, show yourself that you love your long beautiful body.

Position 2 - Stretching Your Legs

While you sit on the floor, cross your legs and push down on your knees with your hands. It feels good. In just a short time, you will experience improved flexibility. In a couple of weeks, you will be able to press your knees down close to the floor. If your muscles are not appreciated and loved, they do not work well.

Position 3 - Calves

I am leaning against the wall stretching my calves. I am lying on the ground pulling my legs straight up in a wonderful stretch. It feels so good. The attention is key. Do not rush when you walk. When we rush, we cannot appreciate the current moment. Practice walking heel to toe. It is a powerful exercise for building up calf muscles. Swing your arms naturally, as you meander and strut through life.

The guides like us to stretch in the sun, standing barefoot, in order to take in all the power from mother earth and the heavens. Stretch very slowly and easily. Stretch all of your joints, even all your little knuckle joints. They say we are in pain because we are tight. Stretching can help.

Movement

Movement of our bodies is important. As mentioned, Costada reminds us that the body is a gift from God through which we are able to enjoy this wonderful life experience. Part of this experience is movement – our ability to move our body, and all of its parts – eyes, arms, legs, fingers, toes, vocal chords, lips, to name a few – in so many various ways that bring us joy, health, happiness and love. We should always be grateful for this gift and love it totally – physically and spiritually. We should infuse our bodies and all of our muscles with love by moving in any way we can – jumping, stretching, dancing, playing, seeing, kissing, etc. We should simply use our bodies the way they were meant to be used – to live life as we know it in this dimension with all of its delightful and marvelous experiences.

Many people think about improving their health, especially as they age. For our emotional health, we see psychiatrists. These doctors pay attention to the brain but some doctors tend to neglect the body. If your body is ill, it affects your brain. However, it's not an issue because your brain, body and soul can fix most things with the help of your spirit guides. The guides think that people forget about their bodies too frequently or take them for granted. The people that pay attention to their bodies by using it correctly, lovingly, by eating well or maybe working out, tend to be healthier. They have fewer injuries and do not suffer as many illnesses as those with a more sedentary lifestyle.

The best way to move should be the easiest. Stroll and walk heel to toe, freely swing your arms. Walk around and explore your world. Remember to never rush (that doesn't mean it's fine to be late; leave yourself enough time to get to your destination in a relaxed mode). When we rush, we tend to hurt our bodies. When we rush, we do not appreciate the current moment, which is all that matters.

Chapter 25

Play

The most frequent message I used to receive from my guides was to meditate. Now that I do it daily, the most frequent message I receive is to play. The reason our souls decide to take on a body is so we can have an enjoyable adventure in life. The guides love to play and laugh and they greatly encourage us to do the same.

One of the ways we can play is to go into a trance and play cards. Decide how many cards you want to pick, and turn the cards over one by one and see what the messages reveal to you.

When I did this, I picked a card that was white and golden on the front. The message is to dance, play and twirl as often as possible. For some reason, the guides are really into wanting us to dance. Maybe because it is a way to move without jagged motions which can lead to injuring ourselves. I definitely advise you to dance, play and twirl a couple of times a day. This movement is very good for your body as well as your soul. Most of us have to work, and many spend far too much time working. If possible, try to achieve a balance between work and play – if not every day, then every other day. Do what you can to spend more time playing. Try to spend more time in nature. Ideally, walk barefoot, so you can soak up all the wonderful energy that mother earth provides us.

I received a card from Costada. The front had a flower on it. The message was "ways to heal" – we have to keep growing, just like the flower. With age comes wisdom. We cannot stagnate; it is bad for the soul and body. Boredom is a sign that you should stop what you are doing. If you are bored, dance, play and twirl whenever you can.

Next, I received a card from the Arcturians. On the front was a picture of me appearing to run up a rainbow. The message was to slide down the rainbow and have fun. You can make life fun. Do not become upset by annoying everyday issues. Instead, keep exploring. There is so much more to find and learn in this life.

The last card I received was from John. It was made of thin cardboard and there were several holes in it from his beak where he had bitten it. The message was simple, yet profound, and a little repetitive. He just wants everyone to have fun, kind of like Cindi Lauper. Arts and crafts are a great way to have fun. Buy a kit from a craft store and put something together. Buy a ball. Find something that appeals to you and play with it. Get creative.

I believe that is why my life is so much better because I emphasize playing. I even find pleasure in doing everyday chores. I've arranged my life so that I do not have to do things I do not enjoy. Work is the one exception. We all have to do it, it is not always fun but the offset is that we are paid.

Put some effort into thinking about what you would like to do. Make a list of fun activities. Include them in your daily life. Simplify your life at the same time. You are probably doing chores as habits that do not need to be done as frequently. Spend time with friends working on strengthening relationships.

For years, I have been getting messages about making more time for play. I thought I had incorporated it into my life. Then one day I was working with hypnotherapist, Ms. Sylvia Moran, and had the most enjoyable meditation. I met an animal spirit guide. He was a black bear (Ralph) and he was to the west of me. I looked up animal spirit guides and found out the bear is to the west. So he was right where he should be. He had sent the bear I had seen the night before. The bear is here to protect me.

After I met the bear, I noticed that all my Arcturian guides had become very small, just a couple of inches tall, and they were flying all around me in colors of gold and silver. Next, all the little Arcturians were sitting on my shoulders sending me waves of love. They explained to me that the universe is full of life; it is not empty space. It is where all the souls exist.

Then I was very small and riding on my bear's back holding onto his thick fur. He took me for a walk and I was bouncing all over the place. Whenever I am cold, I can call in the bear and he will keep me warm. He will lie on top of me and warm me up. He is not very heavy. Next, he looked at my cold feet. He gently licked them with his tongue and warmed up my feet. It was such a fun experience. Ms. Moran said I had a smile on my face the whole time I was in trance.

A few days later I had a party, and realized there is still much more room in my life for more fun. So set your intentions in the morning, and say, "today will be a fun day". See what happens. Do not forget there is endless room for fun in your life.

Chapter 26

Dehydration and Healing with Water

Water Externally

M y guides have taught me much about healing with nature, in particular, healing with water. Specific healing methods involving water frequently come up in conversation with my guides. Soaking in baths, swimming, gently wading in the water – all these are very positive healing methods. We need water. It is good for our insides and our outsides. Being near flowing water is very positive for the body due to the negative ions it gives off.

If you have an area that hurts, the most natural thing to do is to put it in cold running water of a stream, from a faucet in a tub or sink or any body of water. Cold water can take pain away as it numbs the area. Cold flowing water is very good for small cuts, although socking in hot, salty water is better for infections. Cold water can also be very refreshing if you are hot and dizzy.

Water Internally

When I asked my guides about water and dehydration, this conversation ensued.

First, my guides took me for a walk in the woods. I came across a small, grassy, beautiful glen with a sparkling waterfall. I was told three animals would visit me here.

The first animal was a deer, which was serenely drinking from the pool at the bottom of the waterfall. When I asked about the benefits of water, he said it quenches the parched throat. It also fills up an empty stomach. It's refreshing. The deer was thirsty and had a dry mouth, but no longer. The message was if you have a dry mouth, drink something until you are no longer parched. Dehydration can be very expensive (I was very dehydrated for years and had a dry mouth. My teeth started crumbling and my dental bills were off the charts).

The second animal that joined me in the glen was a chipmunk. He said the benefits of water were immense. He was swimming in the water. He likes it because it cleans and refreshes him. He also just loves getting all the dirt off him. The water is always a good alternative when there is no food. At least the animals can drink. The chipmunk also said it makes his whole body work. He is so little he needs to drink very often or he will die. He doesn't swim very well, but he went into the water because he's attracted to it and because he knows it's the most necessary thing. He is smarter than I am. I didn't feel it was that necessary.

The third animal was a black bear. He was slowly lapping up the water. He needs water to live, but he said water is more important for him to have for his insides than it is for the outside of him. He explained that his body needs water because he uses up so much energy and it must be replaced. He does not have to eat every day, but he has to drink every day. Not as often as the chipmunk, but every day.

The animals are all smarter than we are. They listen to their instincts better than you or I do. You don't need to flood your body with water, but you should take in as much as you desire. Water has always been said to be part of a healthy diet. Our brain needs to be hydrated, our skin needs to be hydrated, and our entire body needs to be hydrated.

Water is also a natural cleanser and flushes out all our dead cells. If we do not drink enough, the water can stagnate in our body tissues. As an example, we wash our hands to get them clean, but we do not think to wash our insides with water by drinking more. Imagine you have a small pool, about the size of your body. Imagine filling it with fresh water. The next day you have three glasses of clean water you add to the pool. Consider how old and dirty the water in the pool would be after a few years. That's your body if you do not drink sufficient amounts of fresh water.

These animals are so smart. They can keep themselves clean with the water. When I asked my guides about water, Costada said I did not drink enough. My body was crying out for water. I should drink enough so my mouth isn't dry. They suggested drinking about two bottles of water a day or a half gallon of Double Helix water. *Double Helix* water can be purchased and added to a gallon of distilled water. It produces stable water clusters which are the building blocks of self-healing. Moreover, the water is eminently drinkable. For the first time in 20 years, I am hydrated.

My guides pointed out that my cells need water. My whole body did. I am now drinking more, thanks to the double helix water, but still not enough. They want me to drink water and not iced tea or soda.

John does not want to go in the water. He just says he's really smart. He drinks whatever he needs to. He likes to say he knows more than I do. Moreover, he is correct. He is more in touch with his body and his instincts.

John is just hanging out at the top of the waterfall, flapping his wings. He is a very big bird. He likes being near the water. He likes to see me drinking the water. My guides tell me to stand under the waterfall and just drink. I can do that in the shower, too.

Costada told me that water gives me health. It is the most important thing and I have a love/hate relationship with it. I have swallowing difficulties and I tend to choke when I drink liquids.

In addition, I never enjoyed the sensation of drinking and I never liked the taste of water because I found it too bland.

The guides did not buy that response, saying that the swallowing issue was not a real problem. I should drink water because it is a nourishing gift from God to all of us. I'm foolish to have forgotten something so major. I thought I could get along without it. Now I see water as beautiful and necessary. I know I owe my positive current drinking habits to the power of the *Double Helix* water.

Chapter 27

Insomnia

Meditation is fabulous for insomnia. This is because a somewhat large percentage of the population falls asleep when they meditate. I cannot tell you the number of people I have helped into a trance who have fallen asleep on me. If you have difficulty sleeping, get into bed, get comfortable, turn off the lights and meditate. It's very important not to move all around. Just get in a comfortable position and stay there. Avoid tossing and turning which will keep you awake.

Technique 1

Amber light is a remedy for insomniacs. It is the blue wavelength light that keeps us awake. The blue light prevents the production of melatonin which we need for sleep. Two hours before you plan on sleeping you should put on an amber light. These light bulbs are available in a hardware store. They also sell amber glasses (some fit over regular glasses) that you should wear if you want to watch TV or read. They keep the blue light waves out. Amber is very sleepy light. If you awaken at night to use the rest room, try not to turn on any bright lights.

Other methods to help sleep include:

- Do not have caffeine after 2pm.
- Do not eat meat for three hours before going to bed, as digestion is one of the more difficult processes the body undertakes.
- Avoid alcohol, as it yields poor quality sleep.
- If you take a nap, finish by 3 pm.

(I want to give special thanks to hypnotist, Mr. Jeffrey Rose, for his help in overcoming my insomnia and introducing me to amber light and the information in Technique 1.)

Technique 2

Lie down and get into a comfortable position. First, focus on your breathing. Feel the air as it enters and leaves your lungs. Notice how you abdomen extends with each exhale. Turn your attention to your scalp and relax all the muscles in your scalp, face, jaw and eyes. Slowly relax each body part, even your little knuckles on your toes. Do not let your mind wander. Just love your relaxed body.

Repeat the exercise, but this time pull in a beautiful color through your head and then take the light down through your body and relax all body parts. Give yourself permission to sleep. You can try to open your eyes but they are so heavy and sleepy, you cannot keep them open. You are actually putting yourself in trance before you fall asleep.

However, it is very important to stay in trance because your brain waves are in theta. A person is in theta during meditation and light sleep. Therefore, you are almost asleep when you are in trance.

Technique 3 - How to safely fall asleep

Get ready for bed, get under the covers and allow your eyes to close, with the intention to fall asleep. Go into a trance. Imagine that you are lying on a magical bed and there are five cubes. Each one has a message on it that will quickly enable you to fall asleep.

One by one read the messages.

When I did it, the first cube said that I should not get up during the night and eat because I'm hungry. Instead, I should eat more at dinner and sleep through the night. The second cube said to lie down on a magical mattress. Inside the mattress are all these balls under your body and they make you want to sleep. The third cube said to snuggle up to my husband. The fourth cube said to do a body scan and relax all my muscles. Doing that will let you drift off to sleep.

The last cube said to take my cat into bed with me. He's very good to sleep next to as he has a calming effect on me. However, petting him for too long keeps me awake. The cube said to look him in the eyes and allow my own eyes to close. Even if you don't have a cat, meditate and tell yourself that your eyes want to close. Try to open them part way, but let them close on their own.

Technique from the Arcturians to help you sleep

It is most important to have a comfortable place in which to fall asleep. Use more blankets if you are cold. I was told to take my heating pad to bed with me to stay warm and help heal the muscle spasms in my back.

Don't worry you if you can't sleep. A person can easily get through a day without having slept. We actually don't need that much sleep every single night. Thus, there is no need to be anxious if you are not sleeping. Knowing this is very empowering and decreases or eliminates the anxiety associated with not sleeping. The Arcturians reminded me about a medical test I once had (to check my seizure activity from epilepsy) where I had to stay awake for a week. I was fine, clear-headed and feeling normal the whole time.

Messages from Costada to help you sleep

She likes me to remember our lives when we both had bodies and lived and loved together. She likes nighttime because I meditate and talk to her, but now I can ask her to put me to sleep. I should never underestimate how lucky I am. Besides, if I can't sleep, there's nothing wrong with getting up at night and doing something fun.

Messages from John to help you sleep

Visualize your guides as I visualize John sitting on the bedroom counter, looking over, and protecting me. This is his job and he is good at it because I've only fallen twice in two years during the night. I used to fall a few times a week during the night. He is pushing his beak up against my hands, as he wants me to pet him. He is such a beautiful bird. He can open up his wings and surround me in a hug. I imagine falling asleep next to his warm body.

What is the best question to ask to get to the root of how to sleep?

Each person's inability to sleep is different in each case. Ponder the thoughts in your mind that keep you awake. What does staying awake do for you? Is it harmful that you cannot sleep?

Aside from self-hypnosis, you may be able to find the answers to these questions by keeping a journal and writing in it just before bed. The basis of the journal should be gratitude where you focus on and write down everything you are grateful for that day. You can also include major negatives. By writing them down, it rids your head from all those circular thoughts. By writing down your worrisome thoughts, you do not have to worry about anything that happened that day and you are better able to fall asleep.

Another way to help you fall asleep is taking a warm bath before going to bed. Let the water run out while you are lying in the tub. This is very relaxing. Just don't get cold. Put an amber light and some music on while you relax in the tub.

Most of us do not need medication to sleep, although there is nothing wrong with taking sleeping medication as directed. My guides recommend that insomniacs see a homeopath, hypnotherapist or doctor.

Chapter 28

Endocrine Issues – Addison's Disease/Adrenal Insufficiency, Thyroid Insufficiency

When I asked Costada the cause of my adrenal insufficiency, she told me that there is something wrong with my pituitary gland and it told my adrenal glands to stop working. The reason I developed the problem was that I was seeing a pain doctor and was getting too many steroid injections as well as steroid infusions for MS flair-ups. The steroids caused my body to stop producing cortisol from my adrenal glands, so I had to take steroids every day to replace the cortisol. In turn, that caused me to gain over 70 pounds. Weight gain should not be upsetting because when the pills are stopped, the weight just comes off.

I stopped taking the steroids and I healed myself. When I asked my guides how I managed to accomplish such a feat, I was told I didn't have to do anything. My body naturally just knows how to heal. Everyone's body knows how to heal naturally.

At times, healing occurs spontaneously. The body is always attempting to heal, but sometimes, we are subject to negative influences and we need outside help. You can recognize the tipping point, but then you should see a doctor if you don't feel better after a day (if you are terribly sick go immediately to your doctor or emergency room). If you have a fever, you should go see a doctor because you might have an infection. Antibiotics are needed for infections.

Costada said people should eat a balanced diet, but should also listen to what their bodies want. She recommends that people with adrenal insufficiency (Addison's disease) supplement their diet with one package of black licorice a day. It has to have licorice extract in it. I had a craving for black licorice for three years. That was basically all I ate. Later my wonderful internist, Dr. Arthur Heller, explained to me black licorice is the one food that can aid cortisol levels. After a few years, my adrenal glands started working again, so I am off steroids and black licorice. My levels are still low, but I don't need to take Hydrocortisol anymore.

Addison's disease is a difficult condition because it robs you of your energy. I would fall asleep all the time. I could not focus. If you are so abnormally tired that your whole life is affected, you may want to have your adrenal glands tested.

The Arcturians want to tell people with Addison's to go see a doctor. My doctor started me on 65mg of hydrocortisol a day, but we were able to cut it back to 7mg a day. The message was that people should know that they can cut back on their medication, but only under the advice of their doctor.

My guides believed that this disease should be included in the book since Addison's is a serious condition and people should not have to live with it and suffer. People can avoid getting adrenal insufficiency from steroid injections; however, I acknowledge it is a very rare side effect. I just receive a lot of steroid epidurals and injections for pain since I am allergic to all opiates.

The symptoms of Addison's disease manifest themselves slowly over several months. They include weight loss, decreased appetite and extreme fatigue. You cannot live a normal life. You have no energy. It's not like being totally wiped out from a hard day. It is a different kind of tired, as if you can't walk from one chair to another.

Thyroid Insufficiency

Some people can have thyroid problems and take medicine for them, but these people don't need to stay on the medicine for life. Twice I was on Synthroid, and twice I took myself off it with my doctor's knowledge. Moreover, my thyroid function returned to normal both times.

Most people need to stay on Synthroid for life. However, I have stopped taking about 15 medications (with the knowledge/advice of my doctors) that I had been told I would need to stay on for life.

Chapter 29

Scleroderma

I have scleroderma with CREST. It is a condition which predominately affects my feet, hands and face. I also have a predisposition to developing it around my heart and lungs. The Mayo Clinic describes it as "a group of rare diseases that involve the hardening and tightening of the skin and connective tissues – the fibers that provide the framework and support for your body. In some people, scleroderma affects only the skin."

You know by now that when I am in pain I go into trance and call in my guides to help me. I was having particular discomfort (to say the least) with my toes. So when I went into trance, I asked my toes what they had to say– it turns out I have very talkative feet! My toes wanted to move and wiggle as toes are supposed to do; however, they were trapped and could not move freely due to this disease. They said, "We're not very happy."

Example of how to Show Love to a Body Part

To make my feet happier, I asked what they wanted and they were very clear; they told me exactly what they want. First, they want lots of air. The best would be for me to go barefoot so the air can circulate around my toes. A simple rub of my nails and my toes with soothing cream or lotion would be great, too, as they feel like they've been forgotten. They would really like a weekly foot massage, and a daily body scan performed with loving intension. Second, shoes are a big issue as my shoes had been hurting my toes. I purchased two pairs that caused them pain. Obviously, they prefer I not wear them again. Instead, my feet told me to wear large soft fuzzy boots – ones that won't slip or where my toes have to be in grip mode to help keep them on with every step, but just to give my toes lots of room to move freely. By the way, socks are also a no-no as well, as my toes want space around them. Therefore, to keep my toes happy, I committed to finding shoes and boots that wouldn't hurt them. I did and they are, so to speak, happy feet! Commit to spending five minutes before you go to sleep rubbing the bottoms of your hard working feet.

What would happen if I didn't listen to my toes? Still in trance, I am reminded that my doctors said amputation was a possibility due to the dystrophy caused by either the scleroderma or my RSD. Apparently, my toes are going to keep on hurting me in order that I pay attention and give them the love they need. I make sure to focus on them in hypnotherapy every week. They also welcome the little warm red healing clouds I imagine encircling all the toes on each foot.

Regarding advice for others with CREST and RSD foot problems, they need to make their toes a priority. Roomy shoes are a must! Keep nails trimmed and apply cream to both nails and toes to keep the skin lubricated and soft. Daily rubbing can help loosen the skin in the toe area so it can possibly detach from the connective tissue (this is the nature of the CREST condition). Doing this can also keep the skin from becoming worse or attaching more. I paid attention to my toes, and my dystrophic nail beds have begun to grow nails once more. Again, surprising my doctors.

The fingers were next. Like my toes, they too wanted attention. Scleroderma is like a prison for my fingers, as the skin does not move freely because the skin is hardened. My fingers suggested I make an energy ball (please see chapter on Skin for how to make an energy ball). In the past, I have had success with an energy ball as it healed the scleroderma symptoms on my fingers for a few weeks. Amazingly, instead of having large swollen looking fingers, the fingers were skinny and the skin wrinkled.

The guides advise me to rub my hands and fingers more frequently to loosen up the skin. This is an act of self-love. The idea of using cream appeals to them. As I do not use hand cream every day, they are not happy. They are looking for me to commit to using hand cream every day.

My hands themselves are also talkative. All work and no play do not make happy hands. They want to dance. They want me to focus on each individual finger. They want me to play itsy-bitsy spider. Just like my toes, my fingers welcome the little red healing clouds I call up during meditation; the clouds surround each one warming it with extra blood.

When I asked my guides about the cause of my scleroderma, they said it seems as though I was not connected or grounded. I used any extra connective tissue in my body because I felt unattached from myself. In a way, the scleroderma was giving me a gift; because of it, I don't have wrinkles on my fingers. I had thought it was a bad condition. However, with understanding and acceptance I can now let it go. The extra cells can now leave. I can help this along by focusing on my fingers, feeling the movement between my skin and fingers. Costada said the cells don't need to be connected anymore because I'm connected myself.

I asked Costada how I could get rid of the scleroderma altogether. She said to ask God. She says I am beautiful with or without having had scleroderma. She loves me that much. I like that she is always holding my right hand. She likes my fingers just the way they are.

My Arcturian guides said that scleroderma is healthy, as it is actually the growing of cells and not necessarily a bad thing. They said I do not need to get rid of it; it just gives me a little extra protection. The visualization and the rubbing action have a positive benefit. I focused on my fingers for 30 seconds and I could feel how the blood was flowing in spurts.

Chapter 30

Script Writing – the Power of the Pen in Healing TMJ Pain and other Conditions

S cript writing is a miraculous technique I discovered which helps me help myself when I am in trance. No one knows you better than you do. What you think, what you want to do, how you feel, how you act, what hurts, how much, what's good and what's bad. Ultimately, you are the one in control. That is what script writing is about – you have the ability to help heal yourself as you work with hypnotherapists in trance to explore the whys and wherefores of certain situations, certain dilemmas, certain thoughts and certain pain with the aid of your own writing. The technique works very well, particularly when I know I do have control over something, or even partial control. By writing down my thoughts and directions about how to fix a certain problem or perhaps to help rid me of a certain pain, I am one step closer to healing. It is then I can give the script to my hypnotherapist who reads my own thoughts and directions back to me while I am in trance. As I hear my self-directives, I know in my heart and mind that I can channel the necessary energy to fix the problem at hand.

Script writing put into practice: TMJ Pain, Teeth Grinding and Falling in the Night

If you grind your teeth at night and/or experience TMJ pain, wearing a night guard can help. Your dentist can provide one for you, but who listens to their dentist? Well, I do, but some people don't. So instead, you can take a more proactive approach. This was important to me. I was tired of the pain, the wear and tear on my teeth and the interrupted sleep, to name a few things.

Nevertheless, whatever the reason, I was determined to stop my annoying teeth grinding. I wrote out my plan of action. I gave it to my hypnotherapist with instructions to read it back to me after putting me in a relaxing trance. My subconscious listened to my words and I absorbed every one. The result was that I was able to overcome grinding my teeth at night while I sleep.

A word of caution when writing your directives: Be aware not to include any negatives because the body does not recognize them in trance. Do not say, "When you are asleep, do not grind your teeth." Instead say, "When you sleep your jaw will be relaxed and your teeth will stay separated. Should your teeth touch they will immediately separate by their own desire. You will sleep deeply, comfortably, and your jaw will remain relaxed". It may take a few sessions of hearing these healing directions while you are in trance, but I have found this to be effective.

However, I wondered why I had been grinding my teeth in the first place. A common reason is emotional tension or anxiety. Therefore, my therapist just asked my teeth directly, "Why?" and the response was that I liked the movement. They came up with a movement alternative, telling me to widen my mouth similar to an animal's yawn. So not only did I end my teeth grinding, but subconsciously I found something helpful – exercising my jaw by opening my mouth and stretching it wide. Both things feel good.

Here is another example of how script writing has worked for me. Who doesn't get up during the night to use the rest room? But when I get out of bed during the night, I walk to the rest room. Previously when I did this I would drift off to sleep while walking (often due to the amount of medication I was on) and would fall to the floor – at times severely hurting myself. I must have fallen over 50 times at night. Again, I decided to take action and help stop this hurtful cycle. I wrote out the following directive:

"When you wake up at night to use the restroom, notice that when you first stand up you will be completely awake. When you get into the bathroom and turn on the light, you will be wide awake, as if it is the middle of the day. You will stay fully wide awake as you leave the restroom and return to bed. When you get into bed and pull the covers over you, you will immediately fall back into a deep, relaxing, restorative sleep."

I told my hypnotherapist, Ms. Heather Zicko, to read the script to me, again while in trance. The first night I was wide awake at night. It worked for a few days; then I started falling asleep again during my nightly trek to and from the bathroom. The script was read to me again and the effects lasted three months. I was able to stay awake. Apparently, I had listened to and absorbed my own instructions which kept me safe at night. A few years ago, I listened to the words in trance for the third time and I have not fallen asleep once during the night since.

Chapter 31

Skin – Rashes, Hair Loss, Shingles, Raynaud's, Seroma and Warts

I asked my guides about our skin and they told me that skin is the material that keeps our insides together and safe. Our skin is our number one defense against illness. Thus when your skin is unhealthy from illness, your defenses are doubly down. The skin, our largest organ, protects us by keeping out bacteria and other germs. In turn, our skin is protected by our aura or the light of our souls.

Everyone has an aura that surrounds them. Through its existence, it helps protect us and demonstrates that we have a presence beyond our skin. Part of the aura's protection is that its healing energy helps to heal the skin on the outside as well as the inside. The key word here is "help". The aura does not heal you alone; again, you are in charge and must be open to the healing energy of your aura. Think of the imaginary healing balls I wrote about to remove pain in the Emotional Healing section or the healing clouds I used in previous chapters. The same principles apply here.

Choose to go into a meditative trance. Call in your guides; accept the aid of your hypnotherapist. Know that you have the ability to control what happens. I am sure you have read that enough times. A universal skin issue is wrinkles. Eventually we all get some. However, the good news is that wrinkles and meditation are connected – in a good way. Think about it. Have you ever seen a wrinkle on a Dali Lama? I have come out of a multi-hour meditation, only to find all my wrinkles all gone. They come back but I know that they are fading with each trance. Interested yet?

Wrinkles are an issue for some not completely grounded people. People in alignment accept their wrinkles as a normal part of themselves and consider them nothing to be bothered with. If you are bothered by wrinkles, I recommend *Immuderm* cream. It is a remarkable wrinkle remover, second best to meditation. Aside from wrinkles, there are many other problems and illnesses relating to skin, some minor and some major.

Rashes

Rashes have many causes. Simply put, a rash exists when the skin becomes inflamed, irritated, and often red and itchy. Sometimes you can have a rash for a long time, an indication that something is wrong and you have to take action to get rid of it. In particular, if a rash leads to broken skin, seek some sort of treatment.

The best way to be free of an external rash is to obtain a medicinal cream from your doctor. Creams can treat fungus, eczema, psoriasis and a variety of skin rash conditions. In addition, creams often provide soothing relief, thus reducing your feeling of stress from the rash. Use the cream to heal from the outside.

You can also heal it from the inside. This is when your aura protects you. Use your aura to push away the rash, the foreign matter in your system. While you are in trance, call up a little red healing cloud and position it around the affected area; give it lots of attention. Doing this allows blood to flow to the area. You have to accept the rash because it is now part of you, but that does not mean it has to stay. When you acknowledge this, you are loving all of yourself.

My guides do not get ill often; hence, they have a thin layer of skin and do not need the protection of thick skin. That is why their appearance resembles a low-wattage light bulb; their faces glow and you can see their aura.

To determine how to get rid of a rash I put my guides around a table. According to Costada, the rash is an attention grabber. A rash should not be ignored. Sometimes rashes should be covered with a band-aid or gauze pad until they get better. The rash heals with attention given on the outside. As each cell returns to health on the outside, it makes them healthy on the inside. According to the Arcturians, it is important to pay attention to one's skin, as it is a visual indicator of what is happening on the inside of our bodies. Skin is like a compass to tell us what is wrong.

The Arcturians do not advise using either olive oil or butter as a healing aid for skin problems. Both have a thick consistency and this prevents the skin from breathing. These items can also attract bugs. Alternatively, the Arcturian guides recommend mineral oil or baby oil for especially bad rashes, accompanied by cracked skin. Apply the cream slowly and lovingly. Think about the attention you are giving yourself as you smooth the cream over your skin. Let the skin know underneath that it is loved and then the rash can go away. Skin problems can also often lead to infection, which can slow down healing and can leave a scar. The guides suggest keeping the skin area clean and using antibacterial bandages.

Psoriasis

The following is an example of how to treat psoriasis from both the inside and the outside, using hypnosis as well as common sense. Psoriasis is a skin disorder that can be either mild or severe. Severe psoriasis can lead to serious pain in the inflamed skin as well as in the joints. Go into trance and ask your skin why the psoriasis has appeared? Is it due to a psychological issue (a particularly irritating day at work has you frantic) or is it physical? What does it want? Through your spirit guides, you will receive the answer, most likely that it wants to go away and merely wants your attention. As an exterior solution, put baby oil or cream on the affected area, whichever helps you more.

After a few days of attending to your skin problem, it should start looking better because of all your love and attention. If you have bandaged the skin, take the bandage off and clean the area before you go to bed. Apply more medicine if needed. Re-apply a gauze pad, band-aid or perhaps go without a bandage to let the area breath, depending on what it craves. You will want one thing more than another. Your guides will send you messages from your skin as well.

Scars, Vanity

Depending on the specific problem concerning your skin, there may be a scar after the area heals. You should not be upset about a scar. No one should think worse of themselves because of a scar on their skin. The guides think this type of thinking is stupid (this was the first time they ever used that word). They say that skin is mixed up with vanity, but they think that is wrong. Skin is just an organ. You probably do not spend time thinking about what your liver looks like, so why focus on your skin? People will know and be attracted to you for your whole being, of which skin is only one part. Do you really want a relationship based on one's looks?

When I asked my guides how a person could prevent scars from forming they said there is nothing wrong with having a scar. They do not think they are bad or ugly. According to the guides, your scars should be considered badges of honor because you have gone through the healing process. Many small scars disappear after 6-9 months.

If you are someone who prefers not to have a scar, you might want to change your way of thinking because you cannot prevent it from forming. Scars appear when damaged skin begins to mend as our body creates new fibers. This is just the way we heal. Have pride. No one will think less of you or look at you differently because of a scar. I have no memory of seeing a scar on a person. Do you?

Hair Loss

Losing your hair is a skin condition. Our hair is a remnant from when we had long hair all over our bodies (think cave man days). Losing your hair would not be an issue if we only lived into our teenage years. According to the guides, as we age, sometimes the hair follicle just heals and the hair falls out. It happens naturally over time. It is not a bad thing; the hair has served its purpose. People should not be upset when their hair falls out; it is the natural course of life. Costada said people spend too much time focusing on their hair and skin; instead, they should focus on their souls.

Shingles

I am qualified to speak about shingles because an infectious disease doctor said that I held the world record, having had chicken pox and then shingles seven times (I have a weak immune system).

Shingles is a painful skin rash caused by the varicella zoster virus. If you have had chicken pox, you have it in your body (inactive). When you are an adult (usually over 50) and get an outbreak, it appears in the form of shingles. It is a viral infection and it is treated with anti-viral medication.

The most important thing to know about shingles is that hours matter. This is a disease you need to take control over. If you find a blister or small round burn on your body, and you have not been cooking, take it seriously. Over the next hour, you might see a few more appear. Go right to your doctor or urgent care center. As soon as you start taking the medicine, it stops the disease in its tracks and you are better in a few weeks. However, if you wait a day, it can become a large painful condition that can last a year.

Raynaud's Disease – Energy Balls

Raynaud's is an annoying condition where the blood flow to your fingers and toes is weak. So the digits get very cold and turn purple and then white. I am taking medicine for my circulation problems, but the guides are advising against it. As a type of hand therapy, they want me to enjoy playing with molding clay rather than just using it just as an exercise. Of course, we all agree that a hand massage would feel good.

By accident, I found that one way to help my Raynaud's is to make an energy ball. Begin by standing up with feet shoulder width apart. Stand tall and rub your two hands together. Focus on just the feeling of your skin. Then place your hands very close together but not touching. Feel the warmth and energy from each hand. Then take this energy and make it into a ball by moving your fingers and hands around. Feel the energy as you make it into a little ball.

Next, make the ball larger, like an apple. Then make it even larger to the size of a grapefruit. In addition, just play with the power ball you created. Enjoy the feeling of the energy. We all have this positive healing energy inside us at all times. Take the energy ball and place it anywhere on your body that hurts or put your hands with the energy ball to your face.

The first time I did this, I placed the energy ball to my face. I was amazed that my wrinkles disappeared for a few days. In addition, even more amazingly, my Raynaud's and scleroderma on my hands got better for about a week.

Costada's Technique for Raynaud's Cold Hands:

This is a wonderfully gentle way to bring blood back into your hands and feet. Rather than holding them in warm water, which can cause the skin to dry out, use gravity. Lay on the edge of the bed and if your hand or fingers are white or purple, take one arm and hang it over the bed. You whole body is on the bed but your hand is one the ground. Wait a few minutes, and suddenly you will feel the blood and warmth return to the fingers, thanks to gravity. Then turn around and do the other arm.

She stresses how important it is to keep your hands moisturized. She wants everyone to use hand cream regularly. (She is very practical for a higher being.)

Seroma

When I had squamous cell cancer, they removed a large cancerous piece of me from my thigh to my hip, removing my lymphatic system, the surrounding tissue and over 20 lymph nodes. At the bottom of the incision, I developed a seroma, a large, three-inch, fluid-filled, soft lump, which I had for a couple of years. The doctors did not want to put a needle in it to drain it because they did not want to break the skin, as healing without lymph nodes is a very slow process.

One day I went into a trance and imagined bringing blood to the area to heal it. Then I filled it up with love and imagined the seroma going away, being absorbed into my body in love. After I meditated, about 20 minutes later, I took a shower. I was shocked when I saw this large flab of skin hanging off my leg. Then it dawned on me that the seroma was gone. Shortly thereafter, the flab of skin disappeared as well.

Warts

I happened to be somewhat of an expert on warts. When I had metalized squamous cell cancer, I had a wart on my knee. All warts are the human papilloma virus (HPV). When they could not find the origin of my cancer, my dermatologist sent in a biopsy of my little wart, and it came back as high risk, precancerous. Before me, they did not know common skin warts could cause cancer.

Warts are the easiest thing to fix with meditation. Most of the acid products that are sold to fight warts work in part by being so toxic that they wake up the body to the presence of the wart. Therefore, all you need to do is go into a trance and focus on the wart. Our bodies can heal warts, just as our bodies heal after a cut. Next, imagine the wart disappearing into your skin and just being taken away in your blood stream, all safely. There is no reason that the wart will come back. I saw a podiatrist for nine months to get rid of a planter's wart. Then after one meditation, it was completely gone in three days.

Skin is a very sensitive part of our bodies. Yet it is knocked around a lot; we bump into furniture and bruise our hips, we fall on the sidewalk and scrape our knees or maybe our fingers are burned while we are cooking dinner (I speak from experience on all counts). We expose it to too much sun, making it sore and red, or to too much cold on the ski slopes, making it dry and chaffed. It is also the most important part of our body as it is protects us in many ways from pollution to sensing harmful temperatures to keeping the water within our bodies. We should be thankful for this wonderful skin in our lifetime.

At times, we may find fault with our skin, as we may not like the way it changes over time. When we are in our teens, a pimple on our face can be devastating. Kids can be unkind about looks that are not perceived as the norm for cute or beautiful. Later on, wrinkles show up, we lose our hair, and scars appear. Through hypnosis, we can learn to accept our exterior and all that comes with it, while also learning how to best care for it while we are here in this dimension. Through hypnosis and my spirit guides, I have learned to love my body more and more.

Chapter 32

Life's Goal

I asked Costada what my goal in life should be. She said I already have everything I need to find it within my grasp. She sent me birds with messages about my life's goal. First came a seagull. He told me I can fly wherever I want and that wherever I am is where I want to be. It makes so much sense. I don't have to think about going someplace else. What a smart bird.

The second bird was tiny and bright yellow. He told me I have so much power inside me. So of course, we can heal ourselves with that power. He is a very little bird, but he is very powerful too. We cannot underestimate the amount of power we have that allows us to fix and heal ourselves. We just have to tap into it. The guides say I am doing a good job now. I just have to share the information with others. This is why I chose to write this book and trained as a hypnotherapist; I wanted to be able to help others into a trance and introduce them not only to their spirit guides but to healing methods for their physical and emotional issues.

Setting Your Intentions

We are all in control of our thoughts and you can choose to change them. Emotions are related to thoughts, but are distinctly different. Some thoughts trigger emotions or feelings; some thoughts may not result in any feelings at all. As you go through life you can change the way you choose to feel by setting your intentions. Intentions are different from goals, as the latter helps you focus on the future by planning how to achieve a certain outcome, i.e., becoming a nurse, or perhaps to get to a specific place, i.e., making partner in a law firm. Intentions, however, make you concentrate on your feelings in the moment. They make you think of the values you have in life and what is important to you. They can help steer you down the correct path in life, which can in turn help you achieve your goals.

Practice setting intentions. When you first wake up in the morning say, "Today I want to feel happiness (or joy, love, bliss)." You must be open and receptive to experiencing these feelings and then you will. My days are completely different when I remember to set my intensions in the morning. I cannot stress enough how powerful setting your intensions can be in terms of improving your outlook and your day. You need to do this every morning, as unfortunately it doesn't continue into the next day.

Life can be fabulous when you are on your correct life path. When you set objectives for yourself, you can then be proud when you accomplish your goal. Set intentions so that you can live your life according to the values you believe in. Spend some time determining your life's goal. My guides said a good aim for one's life should be to live in the present moment, surrounded by a halo of love.

Chapter 33

Summary

W hen I finished this book, and submitted it to the editor, I felt a sense of pride in accomplishing a task. Then I meditated and Costada said I should write one final chapter, a summary of what will happen to people when they start meditating and meeting their spirit guides.

The Arcturians say that self-love is the key to changing one's life. The self-love will come about naturally, as your love from your guides grow. When you hit upon an important insight, your whole body will tingle. Self-love really is the closest one can get to themselves and to God.

Costada also said I should tell people to see a hypnotherapist every week. You will be amazed at the progress you will make. A hypnotherapist will help ease you into a trance. You will be asked questions, which in turn you can ask of your guides. One of the most wonderful benefits of this experience is that you will meet your spirit guides, the souls who are always with you. They will share with you their wisdom and endless love and help you overcome both emotional and physical issues.

Costada wants to stress that people should not be so hard on themselves as they go through their lives. A very important lesson is to know that nothing we do is wrong, aside from any violent action. This doesn't mean we are always correct. Quite simply, it just is. When you have completely absorbed this lesson, your life will improve.

Commit to listening to your body when you do body scans in the beginning of each meditation. Then do the best you can in terms of what your guides recommend. Focus on being gentler to your body. Also, slow down. Live in the moment. Know that you have an eternal soul and loving spirit guides with you at all times. You are loved and wanted. How much luckier could we be?

About the Author

K ate Blecher holds an undergraduate degree in economics from Barnard College, Columbia University (1981) and was certified as a professional hypnotherapist in 2013 from the International Association of Counselors and Therapists (IACT). These two seemingly diverse careers occurred during her 30-plus years of immersion and ongoing exploration of self-hypnosis and by connecting, learning, and recording messages from her spirit guides.

Kate began a career on Wall Street as a security analyst in 1981 at Oppenheimer & Co, Inc. Forever curious, she excelled at researching data, interviewing senior bank management, estimating earnings, and providing the brokerage firms' investment options for the major US banks. Throughout her career, Kate was among the top financial services analysts in the country and was named a *Wall Street Journal* All-Star Analyst.

In her most recent work before retirement, Kate was a Vice President at Brown Brothers Harriman & Co., and a managing director at Sandler O'Neill Partners, LP. She retired at age 40, less than a month before September 11, 2001. The day of the September attacks, where she worked at Two World Trade Center on the 104th floor, 68 of her coworkers perished and returned to their true home.

While Kate adored the work, the long hours and constant travel took a toll on her physical body, wherein she entered her second career as a professional patient. She excelled in this field as well, picking up well over 40 medical titles (diseases/conditions). Working with her guides and other master healers, Kate further expanded and honed her healing skills, which helped her deal with four terminal conditions.

In 2003, Kate founded Kate's Holistic Healing, Inc. As a certified hypnotherapist, she works with an adult population. Her area of expertise is working with clients who have acute/chronic medical and emotional conditions. Through hypnotherapy, clients are taught to use their own bodies' natural power to heal. Hypnotherapy is simply a miraculous, natural way to return the body to its proper healthy state with only wonderfully, unexpected side effects.

As a born and bred New Yorker, Kate remains in Manhattan, but splits her time between Manhattan and her house in Pawling, New York. She lives with her wonderful husband Tony and their cat. Her life's path has been to learn, teach, and help others. She loves the energy created when working with clients, reintroducing clients to their guides, and when communicating with her spirit guides. In recent years, she has been channeling messages for herself as well as others from the Arcturians. Her biweekly television show, "Kate's Holistic Healing," can be seen on channel 56, MNN2 on Mondays at 2:30pm EST. Past episodes and meditations can be seen on You Tube under Kate's Holistic Healing. If you would like to see a hypnotherapist, you can visit our website, Katesholistichealing.com, where we have numerous certified hypnotherapists and hypnotists listed under *Professionals.*

The following is a partial list of Kate Blecher's medical conditions/ illnesses:

Metastatic non-Hodgkin's lymphoma
Metastatic squamous cell cancer of unknown origin (left pelvis and leg)
Multiple sclerosis
Scleroderma with CREST
Reflex sympathetic dystrophy (RSD)
Traumatic brain injury (TBI)
Melorheostosis (bone tumor in arm, hand, wrist, elbow, leg)
Retrolisthesis
Failed spinal fusion
Spinal canal stenosis
Anxiety and depression
Chronic pain syndrome
Epilepsy
Addison's disease
Lymphedema
Cecil bascule
Gastrointestinal issues (open valves and swallowing difficulties)
Degenerative disk disease (seven-disc herniations)
Numerous fractures resulting from falls
Metabolic bone disease
Staph infection and recurring cellulitis
Syncope (orthostatic hypotension)
Neurogenic bladder
Spastic urethra
Implanted electronic stimulator
Optic neuritis
Episcleritis
Hiatal hernia

Muscle atrophy
Chronic lymphocytic thyroiditis
Visual distortion
Asthma
Chronic obstructive pulmonary disease (COPD)
Shingles

Printed in the United States
By Bookmasters